Dans la même collection :

Ray Bradbury
A Story of Love
The Last Circus, Stories and Interviews
The Martian Chronicles

Agatha Christie
A Fruitful Sunday and Other Short Stories
The Actress and Other Short Stories

Roald Dahl
Someone like you and Other Short Stories
The Hitch-Hiker and Other Short Stories

Graham Greene
The Third Man

James Joyce
Dubliners

Ruth Rendell
Walter's Leg and Other Short Stories

Ouvrages collectifs
Thirteen Modern English and American Short Stories
English Ghost Stories
English Crime Stories of Today
The Umbrella Man (premières lectures)

Collection « Lire en anglais »
dirigée par Henri Yvinec

Mary Higgins Clark

Terror Stalks
the Class Reunion

Annotations par Henri Yvinec

Le Livre de Poche

Cette nouvelle est extraite du recueil
The Anastasia Syndrome and Other Stories.
© 1989 by Mary Higgins Clark.
© Librairie Générale Française, 2002, pour la présentation et les notes.

ISBN : 978-2-253-08691-8 – 1ʳᵉ publication LGF

Sommaire

Abbreviations

adj	adjective
adv	adverb
Am	American English
cf	confer (see)
fam	familiar
fig	figurative (meaning), *figuré (sens)*
n	noun
plur	plural *(pluriel)*
qqch	*quelque chose*
qqn	*quelqu'un*
sb	somebody
sing	singular *(singulier)*
sl	slang *(argot)*
sth	something
v	verb
=	synonym
≠	antonym or different meaning from expected or not to be mixed up with
« ... »	indicates a word in the text

La collection « Lire en anglais »

Tout naturellement, après quelques années d'étude d'une langue étrangère, naît l'envie de découvrir sa littérature. Mais le vocabulaire dont on dispose est souvent insuffisant ; la perspective de recherches lexicales multipliées chez le lecteur isolé, la présentation fastidieuse du vocabulaire, pour le professeur, sont autant d'obstacles redoutables. C'est pour tenter de les aplanir que nous proposons cette collection. Elle constitue une étape vers la lecture autonome, sans dictionnaire ni traduction, grâce à des notes facilement repérables.

Le lecteur trouvera :

En page de gauche

Des textes de grands auteurs contemporains, pour la plupart, choisis pour leur intérêt littéraire et la qualité de leur langue.

En page de droite

Des notes juxtalinéaires rédigées dans la langue du texte, qui aident le lecteur à :

Comprendre

Tous les mots et expressions difficiles contenus dans la ligne de gauche sont reproduits en caractères gras et expliqués dans le contexte ;

Observer

Des notes d'observation de la langue soulignent le caractère idiomatique de certaines tournures ou constructions ;

Apprendre

Dans un but d'enrichissement lexical, certaines notes proposent enfin des synonymes, des antonymes, des expressions faisant appel aux mots qui figurent dans le texte.

C'est à dessein que quelques mots clés sont expliqués plus d'une fois. Ils sont alors présentés sous un autre angle, notamment à l'aide de nouveaux synonymes ou antonymes, plus adéquats dans un nouvel épisode de l'histoire. Ceci pourra également éviter des retours en arrière toujours fastidieux.

Vocabulaire en contexte

En fin de volume une liste importante de mots contenus dans le texte, suivis de leur traduction, comporte, entre autres, les verbes irréguliers et les mots qui n'ont pas été annotés faute de place ou parce que leur sens était évident dans le contexte. Grâce à ce lexique, on pourra, en dernier recours, procéder à quelques vérifications ou faire un bilan des mots retenus au cours des lectures.

Henri Yvinec

About Mary Higgins Clark

Born and brought up in New York, Mary Higgins Clark is of Irish descent. 'The Irish are, by nature, storytellers,' says 'the queen of suspense,' who considers her Irish heritage an important influence on her writing.

Mary Higgins Clark's father died when she was ten years old. Her mother struggled to raise the novelist to be and her two brothers. After graduating from high school, Mary Higgins Clark went to secreterial school in order to get a job and help her mother with the family finances. After working for three years in an advertising agency, travel fever seized her. For the year 1949, she was a stewardess on Pan American Airlines. 'My run was Europe, Africa and Asia,' she recalls. 'I was in a revolution in Syria and on the last flight into Czechoslovakia before the Iron Curtain went down. I flew for a year and then got married.'

She married a neighbour, Warren Clark. Nine years her senior, she had known him since she was sixteen. Soon after her marriage, she started writing short stories. She sold her first story to *Extension Magazine* in 1956 for a hundred dollars, after six years and forty rejection slips. 'I framed that first letter of acceptance,' she recalls.

Mary Higgins Clark was left a widow with five children by the death of her husband from a heart attack in 1964. She went to work writing radio scripts and, in addition, decided to write books.

Every morning, she got up at five o'clock and wrote until seven, when she had to get the children ready for school. Her first book was a biographical novel about the life of George Washington, *Aspire to the Heavens*. Next, she decided to write a suspense novel *Where are the Children ?*, which became a bestseller and marked a turning point in her life and career.

Then she decided to take time for things she had always wanted to do. So far, she had put all her energies into her children's education. Now she was going to catch up on her own. In 1974, she entered Fordham University at Lincoln Center in New York and graduated in 1979 with an honours degree in philosophy.

After many years of widowhood, she married John J. Conheeney in 1996. They now live in Saddle River, New Jersey.

Among the many honours she has received, Mary Higgins Clark was awarded France's Grand Prix de Littérature policière in 1980. She is a number one bestseller in France. Her books are published in translation around the world, among which, *While My Pretty One Sleeps ; All Through the Night ; Weep No More, My Lady ; Death on the Cape and Other Stories...* and of course *A Stranger is Watching (La Nuit du renard)*, 'not to be read alone at night,' as *Cosmopolitan* had it.

Terror Stalks the Class Reunion, typical of the way Mary Higgins Clark handles suspense, is taken from a collection of short stories entitled *The Anastasia Syndrome*, a bouquet of surprise, romance and spellbinding tension. Enjoy yourselves.

Terror Stalks the Class Reunion

Terror Stalks the Class Reunion

He watched Kay from the corner of his eye. For these three days he'd been careful to stay away from her, never to be caught in a group picture with her. It hadn't been difficult. Nearly six hundred alumni had turned out for this reunion. For three days he'd had his nerves twisted as they'd launched into the tiresome memories of silly school-kid nonsense from their days together at Garden State High in Passaic County, New Jersey.

Kay had finished eating a hot dog. She must have felt something on her lip because she brushed it with her fingertip, then laughed and poked the fingertip in her mouth. Tonight he would hold those fingers in his own hands.

He was standing at the edge of a group. He knew that the weight he had lost in these eight years, the beard he had grown, the contact lenses instead of the heavy glasses, the bald spot under his thinning hair, had changed his appearance a lot more than most of the students'. But some things didn't change. Not one person had come up to him and said, 'Donny, great to see you.' If anyone had recognized him, they'd rushed past. Just like the old days. He could see again the school cafeteria when he'd bring the sandwich in a paper towel and go from table to table. 'Sorry, Donny,' they'd mumble, 'no room.'

Finally he'd come to the point where he'd sneak onto the fire escape stairs and eat his lunch there.

But now he was glad that in these three days no one had slapped his back or clasped his arm or yelled, 'Great to see you.' He'd been able to drift on the edges of groups, able to watch Kay, able to plan what he would do. In exactly one half hour more she would belong to him.

stalks: affects, haunts ► **class reunion**: meeting of 'alumni' (students who have left school the same year and enjoy getting together again); the **class** of '82'

watched: looked attentively at
... careful: done his best ► **to stay away**: not to mix with
caught: (here) photographed ► **a picture**: a photography
nearly: almost ► **alumni**: see above (sing. alumnus) ►
turned out: come (in great numbers)
twisted: distorted ► **launched...**: started talking about ► **tiresome memories**: uninteresting remembrances ► **silly**: stupid
Garden State High (secondary school) ► **County** (administrative division of a state)
brushed: removed with a quick movement
fingertip: tip (extremity) of finger ► **poked**: pushed
hold: have and keep

edge: side≠middle, centre (not mixing with anybody)
weight (of a person's body in kilos...) ► lose, lost, **lost**
beard: hair on face ► **grown**: let develop ► **lenses** (to see better)
heavy: big ► **bald spot**: hairless space ► **thinning**: getting thin, rare ► **most of**: the majority of
the students' (appearance)
great: super! wonderful!
rushed past: walked past rapidly without paying attention to him
the old days (when he was at school)
he'd bring: he was in the habit of bringing
paper towel: piece of paper (in which the sandwich is wrapped)
mumble: speak indistinctly ► **no room**: no seat left for you
sneak: go furtively
fire escape stairs: metal staircase on exterior of building
glad: pleased
slapped (with palm of hand) ► **clasped**: seized ► **yelled**: (in a loud voice) ► **drift**: move in a slow casual (nonchalant) way
plan: make plans (projects) about
one (to be precise); one≠a, an
belong to him: be his

'What class were you?'

For a moment he wasn't sure that the voice was questioning him. Kay was sipping a soda. She was talking to a student who had graduated in Donny's class, Virginia something or other. Kay's honey-coloured hair was brighter than he'd remembered. But she lived in Phoenix now. Maybe the sun had streaked it. She'd cut it so that it curled around her face. It used to lie on her shoulders. Maybe he'd make her let it grow again. 'Kay, let your hair grow. Your husband is laying down the law.' He'd be teasing but he'd mean it.

What was the stupid question this stupid person had asked? Oh–the year he graduated. He turned. Now he recognized the man, the new principal. He'd made the opening remarks on Tuesday. 'I graduated eight years ago,' Donny said.

'That's why I don't know you. I've just been here four years. I'm Gene Pearson.'

'Donny Rubel,' he mumbled.

'It's been a fantastic three days,' Pearson said. 'Terrific attendance. Great school spirit. At a college you expect it. But high school... It's wonderful.'

Donny nodded. He blinked and made it seem that he was moving because the sun was in his eyes. He could see that Kay was shaking hands with people. She was going to leave.

'Where do you live now?' Pearson seemed determined to keep up the conversation.

'About thirty miles from here.' To forestall any more questions Donny said hurriedly, 'I have my own fix-it business. My van is my workshop. Go anywhere up to an hour's drive to do repairs. Well, good to meet you, Mr Pearson.'

'Say, maybe you'd want to talk at our career day. Kids need to know there are alternatives to college...'

Donny raised one hand as though he hadn't heard. 'Gotta run. Some of the guys from my class and I are pushing on to dinner.' He didn't give Pearson a chance to answer. Instead he began to skirt the picnic area.

moment: brief space of time
sipping: drinking in repeated small quantities
graduated: obtained her degree or diploma
honey-coloured: the colour of honey (made by bees flying from flower to flower) ► **bright(er)**≠dark
Phoenix, Arizona ► **streaked**; streak, mark (of brighter colour, here) ► **curled**: curved upwards; curled hair≠straight hair

laying down the law (expecting obedience!); law, rule
teasing: assailing her with jokes ► **mean it**: really expected her to obey
turned (without a reflexive pronoun!)

the opening remarks or speech on the first day of the reunion (quite a big affair in the USA; it lasts three days here!)

terrific (fam): wonderful, excellent
attendance: number of people present ► (university) **college** (senior) **high school** (here)≠junior high school
nodded: moved his head as a sign of assent ► **blinked**: moved his eyelids quickly up and down
shaking hands with people (before leaving them)
leave, left, left: go away
determined: firm, resolute
keep up the conversation: continue...
about: approximately ► **forestall...**: prevent him from asking more questions ► **hurriedly**: (too) rapidly
fix: repair ► a **van** is bigger than a car ► **workshop** (to work in)
up... drive: in so far as it takes an hour to go by car ► **meet** (for the first time): make the acquaintance of
say (used to attract attention) ► **career day** (when students are given information about jobs or careers)
raised (in an upright position) ► **as though**: as if
gotta run (Am): I've (got) to run ► **guys** (Am): boys <u>and</u> girls
pushing on to (fam): going to ► **chance**: opportunity
instead: in lieu of that ► **skirt**: move along the border of

He'd dressed carefully, khaki slacks, a blue polo shirt. Half the guys here had on practically the same thing. He'd wanted to blend into the crowd, be as inconspic- uous as he'd been conspicuous in the years he'd spent in this school. The only kid in the class who wore an overcoat when everyone else had a school jacket.

Kay was walking through the grove of trees that separated the picnic area from the parking lot. The school adjoined the county park, so ideal for the re- union. And so ideal for Donny. He caught up with her just as she opened her car door. 'Miss Wesley,' he said. 'I mean, Mrs Crandell.'

She looked startled. He knew that in a minute the parking lot would be crowded. He'd have to hurry. 'I'm Donny Rubel,' he said. 'I guess you don't rec- ognize me.'

She looked unsure, then that smile that he'd envision- ed so many times lying awake at night began to form. 'Donny. How good to see you. You look so different. Have you been here long? How come I haven't seen you?'

'Just made it here,' he explained. 'You're the only one I wanted to see. Where are you staying?'

He already knew. The Garden View Motel on Route 80. 'That's perfect,' he said when she answered. 'A car is picking me up there in half an hour. I cabbed over. Is there any chance you could drop me? It would give us a chance to talk.'

Did she suspect something? Was she remembering that last night when she told him she wasn't coming back next term, that she was going to be married, and he'd started to cry? She hardly hesitated, then said, 'Of course, Donny. It will be good to catch up. Hop in.'

He managed to bend down and yank his shoelace open as he hurried around to the passenger side. When he got into the car he leaned over and made a big thing of tightening the shoelace. Anyone who noticed the car at all would swear Kay had left the picnic area alone.

Kay drove swiftly. She tried to push down her faint

slacks (covering legs**)**: trousers for sport, games...
had on: were wearing (clothes)
blend: mix ▶ **crowd**: lots of people ▶ **inconspicuous**: not attracting attention, not easily seen (≠conspicuous)
wear (clothes), **wore**, worn
overcoat (worn over a jacket) ▶ **everyone else**: all the others
grove: group of trees
parking lot (Am): car park
adjoined: was contiguous to
caught up with: came up to her (after hurrying)

I mean (to say) (correcting himself)
looked: seemed ▶ **startled** (as if she was given a shock)
crowded: full (see 'crowd') ▶ **hurry**: be quick
I guess (Am): I suppose, I think

unsure: hesitant ▶ **smile** on face showing joy ▶ **envisioned**: imagined ▶ **awake**≠sleeping ▶ **form**: become visible (here)
good to see you: nice to see you
how come?: how is it that? why?

just made it here: I have only just arrived
stay(ing) (at a hotel...)
motel (Am): roadside hotel for motorists
Route 80 (Am) (major road between major cities)
picking me up: taking me in (as a passenger) ▶ **cabbed**: came in a cab (taxi) ▶ **drop me**: take me in your car and leave me there

that last (≠first) **night** (evening)
next: coming immediately after ▶ (school) **term**: 3 months
cry (with tears in his eyes, being unhappy) ▶ **hardly**: *à peine*
catch up: learn the latest news about each other ▶ **hop in**: (fam) get into the car ▶ **managed to**: succeeded in ▶ **bend down** (inclining his body) ▶ **yank...open**: quickly undo
leaned over: bent down ▶ **made... thing of** (to perfection, in an exaggerated way) ▶ **tightening**≠undoing, yanking open; tight, firm≠loose ▶ **swear**: say solemnly, with emphasis ▶ **alone**: by herself ▶ **swiftly**: rapidly ▶ **push down**: control ▶ **faint**≠strong

irritation at the presence of the young man beside her. Mike would be home from New York in an hour and after the way she'd been so rotten to him on the phone last night, she was desperately anxious to straighten things out between them. This school reunion had been good for her. It had been fun to see the teachers she'd worked with the two years she'd taught there, fun to catch up with her students. She'd loved teaching. That was one of the problems between her and Mike. His job of setting up new plants for his company meant that they never stayed any place more than a year. Twelve moves in eight years. She'd told him when he'd left her at the motel to tell the company that he wanted a permanent assignment.

'That sounds like an ultimatum, Kay,' he'd told her.

'Maybe it is, Mike,' she'd answered. 'I want roots. I want to have a baby. I want to be in a place long enough that eventually I can get back into teaching. I can't keep moving like this. I just can't.'

Last night he'd started to tell her that the company had promised him a partnership and a permanent spot in the New York office if he would just do one more on-location job. She'd hung up on him.

She was so concerned with her own thoughts that she didn't notice the silence of her passenger until he announced, 'Your husband's been at a company meeting in New York. He's due back tonight.'

'How did you know?' Kay looked quickly at the impassive profile of Donny Rubel, then glued her eyes to the road.

'I talked to people who talked to you.'

'I thought you just got to the picnic.'

'You thought that. That's not what I said.'

The vent was blowing cool air into the car. Kay's skin went suddenly cold as though the pleasant June evening had chilled. They were less than a mile from the motel. Her foot went down on the accelerator. Something warned her not to ask questions. 'It worked out so well,' she said. 'My husband had a business

beside: near

way: manner ▶ **rotten**: (fam) most unpleasant, horrible
anxious: very desirous ▶ **straighten things out**: remove difficulties, worries
fun: pleasure, enjoyment ▶ **she... with**: with whom she had worked ▶ **taught**: past participle of 'teach'
catch up with...: learn what has become of them since they left school
setting up: starting, establishing ▶ **plant(s):** factory, firm
(in) any place (Am): anywhere
move(s): change of residence, removal

assignment: post, position
sounds like: seems to be (as I hear it)
roots: close (intimate) relationship with an environment

eventually: in the end ▶ **get back...**: start teaching again
keep: continue ▶ **moving**: to move, to change residence
last night: yesterday in the evening
partnership (being associated in the business) ▶ **spot**: post

on-location (away from the New York office) ▶ **hung up on him**: suddenly ended the telephone conversation (angrily)
notice: pay attention to, take notice of

he's due back: he's expected to be back

impassive: calm, without emotion ▶ **glued her eyes to the road** (continually, with all her attention); to glue, to stick

just got to the picnic: went only to the picnic (p 16)
think, thought, thought: believe
vent(ilator) ▶ **blowing** (like the wind): sending ▶ **cool**≠hot
skin (covers human body) ▶ **went cold**: became, got cold
chilled: become cold; chilly, unpleasantly cold
went down on the accelerator (in order to drive faster)
warned (as of a danger) ▶ **worked out so well** (just as we wanted, according to our plans)

meeting in New York. I got the notice about the reunion and...'

'I read the *Alumni News*,' Donny Rubel told her. 'It
said, "Garden State High's favourite teacher to come
to reunion." '

'That was generous.' Kay tried to laugh.

'You didn't recognize me.' Donny sounded pleased.
'But I bet you didn't forget you went to the prom with
me.'

She'd taught English and choir. The guidance counsellor, Marian Martin, had suggested that Donny Rubel
join the choir. 'He's one of the saddest kids I've ever
seen,' she told Kay. 'He's a klutz at sports, he has
no friends, I'm sure he's bright but he just gets by
academically, and God knows the poor kid was behind
the gate when looks were given out. If we can get him
in an activity where he might make friends...'

She remembered his earnest efforts, the snickers of
the others in the group until one day when Donny was
out, she'd talked to them. 'I have news for you guys.
I think you're rotten.' They'd let up on him, at least
during choir. After the spring concert he used to drop
in to talk with her. That was when she'd learned he
wasn't going to the prom. He'd invited three girls and
they'd all turned him down. On impulse, she'd suggested that he come anyhow and sit with her at dinner.
'I'm one of the chaperones,' she said. 'It will be nice
to have you with me.' Uneasily she remembered how
Donny had started to cry at the end of the evening.

The motel sign was on the right. She chose not to
notice that Donny's hand had moved and was brushing
her leg.

'Remember at the prom I asked if I could see you
over the summer? You told me you were getting married and moving away. You've lived in a lot of places.
I've tried to find you.'

'You have?' Kay tried not to sound too nervous.

'Yes. I looked you up in Chicago two years ago but
by then you'd moved to San Francisco.'

notice (telling me the reunion was taking place and when)

Alumni News : newspaper for the alumni (former students)
to come: is (due) to come

generous: nice to say 'favourite' ▶ **tried**: did her best
sounded pleased: seemed pleased (satisfied, happy)
I bet: I'm sure ▶ **prom**: (Am): formal dance given by a high school
or college class
choir: singing ▶ **guidance counsellor** (gives students advice as
to the choice of their career)
(should) **join** ▶ **choir**: group of singers ▶ **sad(dest)**: unhappy
he's a klutz (Am) **at**: he's no good at
bright: brilliant ▶ **gets by**: is acceptable but not very good
academically: in his studies ▶ **was behind the gate** (barrier)
when looks (beauty) **was given out** (distributed): is not good-
looking ▶ **make friends**: not 'do'!
earnest: serious ▶ **snicker(s)** (Am): quiet, unkindly laugh (with a
note of mockery)
news: sth to tell you ▶ **guys** (Am) (calling boys <u>and</u> girls)
let up on: treated less severely
drop in: come and see her (without arranging a particular time)
learned (Am): learnt, heard

turned him down: rejected him ▶ **on impulse**: without thinking
he come (subjunctive) ▶ **anyhow**: in any case
chaperone(s): older person who accompanies young people at
a social gathering to ensure proper behaviour ▶ **uneasily**: feeling
ill at ease, uncomfortable
sign (outside a motel... as advertisement) ▶ **chose not to**:
decided not to ▶ **brushing**: touching lightly in passing

over the summer: during the summer
moving away: going away to live in another place
to find, found, found≠to lose, lost, lost
nervous: tense, worried
I looked you up...: I went there, trying to see you
by then: at that time

'I'm sorry I missed you.'

'Do you like to move around so much?' Now his hand was resting on her knee.

'Hey, fellow, that's my knee.' She tried to sound amused.

'I know it. You're really sick of moving around so much, aren't you? You don't have to any more.'

Kay glanced at Donny. The heavy, dark sunglasses covered his eyes and half his face, but his mouth was pursed and partly open. He was exhaling through it now, an almost soundless whistling note that had an eerie echo.

'Drive to the end of the lot and turn left behind the main building,' he told her. 'I'll show you where to park.'

His hand tightened on her knee. She felt before she saw the gun that he pressed against her side. 'I'll use it, you know,' he whispered.

This couldn't be happening. She should never have given him a ride. Her hands trembled as she turned the wheel in obedience to his directions. There was a cold chill in the pit of her stomach. Should she try to attract attention, to crash the car? She heard the click of the safety catch on the gun.

'Don't try anything, Kay. There are six bullets in this gun. I only need one for you, but I won't waste the others. Pull in beside that van, on the other side. The last spot.'

She obeyed him, then realized immediately that her car was totally hidden from the windows of the motel by the dark-grey van on the left. 'Now slide out your door and don't scream.' His hand was on her arm. He slipped out behind her. She heard him pull the key ring from the starter and drop it on the floor. In one quick movement he pushed her forward and slid open the side door of the van. With one arm he lifted her inside and climbed in behind her. The door slid closed. Almost total darkness replaced the late afternoon sun. Kay blinked.

I missed you: I did not see you

resting: lying
fellow (calling him): man, boy

you're sick of: you've had enough of, you're fed up with
you don't have to (move)
glanced at: took a quick look at
half his face: notice the construction!
pursed: contracted ▶ **partly**: not entirely
soundless: hardly audible ▶ **whistling note**: piercing, sharp sound ▶ **eerie**: strange, mysterious, fearful
end: extremity ▶ **lot** (Am): parking lot, car park
main: principal
to park a car, a van, a lorry or truck (Am)...
tightened on her knee: caught her knee more firmly; tight, firm
use: make use of
whispered: murmured
happen(ing): used about an event (not 'arrive'!)
given... ride: taken him in her car; ride, journey in a vehicle
wheel (in her hands to drive the car) ▶ **in obedience...**: obeying his orders ▶ **chill**: cold ▶ **pit**: *creux*
crash: break to pieces through collision ▶ **click**(ing) noise
safety catch (to prevent accidental firing); safety, security
bullet(s) (fired out of a gun)
waste: use unecessarily
pull in: stop ▶ **beside**: near
spot: parking space
obeyed him: no preposition!
was hidden: was not visible; hide, hid, hidden
slide out (of) **your door** (quickly, quietly)
scream: give a loud, sharp (high-pitched) cry
slipped out (quietly, silently) ▶ **key ring** (with the ignition key on it to start the car with) (starter) ▶ **drop**: let fall
forward(s)≠backward(s) ▶ **slid open...** (by moving it along)
lifted her: took her up
climbed in: got up in ▶ **slid closed** (being moved along)
the late afternoon: the end of the afternoon
blinked: moved her eyelids quickly up and down

'Donny, don't do this,' she pleaded. 'I'm your friend. Talk to me but don't...'

She felt herself being pushed forward, stumbled and fell onto a narrow cot. Something was covering her face. A gag. Then with one hand he held her down, with the other snapped handcuffs on her wrists, shackles on her ankles and joined them with a heavy metal chain. He slid open the side door of the van, jumped down, and snapped it closed. She heard the driver's door slam shut and an instant later the van began to move. Her desperate efforts to attract attention by pounding her chained legs against the side of the van were defeated by the clicking of the tires against the macadam.

Mike bit his lip impatiently as the cab driver slowed to allow a van to cross in front of them at the turn-off to the motel. His lean, disciplined body vibrated with tension as he willed the cab to move faster.

He felt lousy about the way he and Kay had left it last night. He'd almost called her back when she hung up on him. But he knew Kay–she never stayed angry long. And now he could give her what she wanted. *Just one more assignment, honey. A year at most... maybe even six months. Then they'll bring me into the New York office permanently as a partner.* If she wanted, they could buy a house in this area. She liked it here.

The driver pulled up to the lobby entrance.

Mike jumped out of the cab. Long strides took him through the lobby.

He and Kay were in room 210. His first reaction when he turned the key and pushed the door open was keen disappointment. It was a little early for Kay to be back but somehow he'd expected to find her. The room was typical motel: shaggy carpeting, beige and brown bedspread, heavy oak-veneer double dresser, television camouflaged in an armoire, windows overlooking the parking lot. The other night he had simply dropped Kay here and rushed off to New York for the first sales

pleaded: asked in an intense and emotional way, begged

stumbled: nearly fell over
narrow≠wide, broad ▶ **cot**: (Am) temporary camp bed
gag (to force her to be silent) ▶ **held...**: made her stay down
snapped (put on abruptly) **handcuffs** (manacles) ▶ **wrist(s)**:
joint between hand and arm ▶ **shackles**: iron rings ▶ **ankl(es)**
joint between foot and leg ▶ **slid open**: opened by sliding
jumped down (quickly) ▶ **snapped...**: closed it quickly
slam shut (violently)

pounding: beating, hitting, striking with great force
defeated: made useless ▶ **clicking** (noise) ▶ **tire(s)** (Am),
tyre (onto the wheels of cars..., full of air)

bit (with his teeth) ▶ **cab driver**: taxi driver ▶ **slowed**: drove more
slowly ▶ **allow**: make it possible for ▶ **turn-off**: place where you
deviate from a main road ▶ **lean**, thin≠fat
willed...: wanted will all his heart the car to go faster
lousy (fam): ill at ease ▶ **had left it**: had left each other
called back: phoned again ▶ **hung up on him**: see p 18
stayed: remained
long: for a long time
honey (fam): darling ▶ **at most**: not more than (a year)

as a: in the capacity of ▶ **partner**, partnership
area: region
pulled up: came to a stop ▶ (hotel) **lobby**: large hall
stride(s): long walking step

pushed... open: opened the door by pushing it
keen: acute, intense ▶ **disappointment**; be disappointed with
one's hopes or expectations
shaggy: (too) long ▶ **bedspread** (over a bed in daytime) ▶ **oak-
veneer**: *plaquage chêne* ▶ **dresser** (Am): *commode-coiffeuse*
armoire (Am): cupboard ▶ **overlooking**: having a view of
dropped her: taken her in his car and left her here
rushed (with speed) ▶ **sale(s)**; to sell≠to buy

meeting. Reluctantly he remembered how Kay had wrinkled her nose and said, 'These rooms. They're all alike and I've been in so many of them.'

And yet, as usual, she had managed to add a touch of homeyness to the place. There were fresh flowers in a vase and next to it three small silver picture frames. One showed him holding a freshly caught striped bass, another was a snapshot of Kay in front of their Arizona condo, the third, a Christmas-card picture of Kay's sister's family.

The books Kay had brought to read were on the night table. The mother-of-pearl comb, brush and hand mirror that had been her mother's were neatly placed on the dresser. When he opened the door of the closet, there was the faint scent of the sachet bags on her satin hangers.

Unconsciously Mike smiled. Kay's exquisite neatness was a continuing source of joy to him.

He decided that a quick shower would feel good. When Kay got back, they'd talk it out and he'd take her for a festive dinner. *A full partner, Kay. Within the year. It's been worth all the moving. I promised you it would happen*. As he hung up his suit and stuffed his underwear and socks and shirt in the laundry bag, the thought struck him that the constant moving had never bothered him because Kay had managed to make a home out of every motel unit or rented apartment they'd ever stayed in.

At six-fifteen, he was sitting at the round table overlooking the parking lot, watching the news and listening for the turn of the key in the lock. He'd set out a bottle of wine from the room bar-refrigerator. At six-thirty, he opened the wine and poured a glass. At seven, he began watching Dan Rather who was reporting a new outburst of terrorist activity. At seven-thirty, he had worked up a self-justifying annoyance... All right, so Kay's still mad at me. If she's having dinner with friends, she could have left a message. At eight o'clock, he called the desk for the third time and was

reluctant(ly): (slow to do sth because) unwilling
wrinkled... (in disgust...); wrinkle, line (on forehead...)
alike: like one another, the same
yet: but still, however ▶ **add**; addition
homeyness (Am): feeling, impression of being at home
next to: near ▶ **silver**, gold... ▶ photographs in **frames**
striped; stripe, narrow band of different colour ▶ **bass** (fish)
a snapshot: a photograph (taken quickly)
condo (Am): block of flats (each being owned by occupant)
▶ **Christmas...**: photograph of family sent as a Christmas card
(a typically American custom)
mother-of-pearl: *nacre* ▶ **comb** (for one's hair)
her mother's (comb...) ▶ **neatly**; neat, well arranged
closet (Am) (for hanging clothes in), cupboard
faint≠strong ▶ **scent**: smell ▶ **sachet bags** (containing perfume
powder) ▶ **hanger(s)** (for hanging clothes)
exquisite: delicate, elegant ▶ **neatness**: see 'neatly' above

just a **shower** not a bath ▶ **feel good**: do him good
talked it out: made peace by talking
festive (to celebrate) ▶ **full**: total, complete ▶ **within...**: before
the end of ▶**... all the moving** was not for nothing
suit: jacket and trousers ▶ **stuffed...**: pushed quickly into
underwear: underclothes ▶ **laundry bag** (for dirty clothes)
thought: idea ▶ **struck him**: crossed his mind (suddenly)
bothered: perturbed, upset, worried
rented: occupied in return for payment ▶ **apartment** (Am): flat,
set of rooms

watching the news (on TV) ▶ **listening for**: expecting to hear
lock (into which key is put) ▶ **set out**: taken out and put on the table

poured a glass (out of the bottle)
Dan Rather, a famous American TV newsreader (newscaster)
outburst: sudden violent period
worked up: developed ▶ **annoyance**: irritation
mad at (Am): mad with, angry with

(reception) **desk** ▶ first, second, **third**, fourth, fifth...

again assured by a testy operator that *there were absolutely no messages for Mr Crandell in room 210*. At
nine o'clock, he began going through Kay's address
book and managed to find the name of a former student
he knew Kay kept in touch with. Virginia Murphy
O'Neil. She answered on the first ring. Yes, she had
seen Kay. Kay left the picnic just when it was breaking
up. As a matter of fact, Virginia had seen Kay drive
away. That would have been between five-fifteen and
five-thirty. She was absolutely sure Kay was alone in
the car.

When he finished speaking to Virginia O'Neil, Mike
called the police to ask about accidents between the
school and the motel and on learning there were none
reported Kay missing.

The handcuffs dug into her wrists; the shackles were
bruising her ankles; the gag was choking her.

Donny Rubel? Why was he doing this to her? She
suddenly thought of Marian Martin, the guidance counsellor who had asked her to take Donny into the choir.
That last week she'd told Marian that she'd invited
Donny to sit at her table at the prom. Marian had been
troubled. 'I've already heard about it,' she said.
'Donny bragged to someone that you asked him to be
your date. I suppose it's understandable, the way the
kids make fun of him, but even so... But, really, what
difference? You're leaving, you're getting married in
two weeks.'

But he's kept track of me all these years. Kay felt
herself panicking. She strained her eyes but could not
see him through the partition. The van seemed unusually wide and in the near darkness she could begin
to make out the outlines of a worktable opposite the
cot. Over it a corkboard held a variety of tools. What
did Donny do with them? What was he planning to do
to her? *Mike, help me, please*.

The road seemed to climb and twist and curve. The
narrow cot swayed, bumping her shoulder against the

testy: irritable, impatient, easily annoyed

going through: examining
former student: alumnus
kept in touch with: was still in contact with
on the first ring (of the telephone): immediately
breaking up: coming to an end
as a matter of fact: in fact, in actual fact
that would have been: that was probably
alone: unaccompanied, on her own, by herself

called: phoned
on learning: as he learnt ▶ **none**: no accident
reported Kay missing: told the police Kay had disappeared

dug...: were pushed into her wrists (and hurt them)
bruising: damaging, hurting ▶ **choking**: suffocating

thought of: notice the preposition!

troubled: perturbed ▶ **heard about it**: learnt about it
bragged (implies self-glorification): said proudly
date (Am): sb you go out with, boyfriend (or girlfriend)
make fun of: mock ▶ **even so**: in spite of that ▶ **what difference**
(does it make?)

kept track... (knowing where I was, what happened to me...)
strained her eyes (making an intense effort to see)
partition: thin wall (made of glass, wood...)
wide: large, spacious ▶ **near darkness**: almost total darkness
make out: see ▶ **outline(s)**: contour, shape
corkboard with tools on it to work with; cork: *liège*
planning; to make plans (for the future)

climb: go up ▶ **twist and curve** (instead of being straight)
swayed: rocked to and fro ▶ **bumping**: knocking, hitting

side of the van. Where were they going? Finally she
sensed that they were descending. More curves, more
bumps and the van stopped.

She heard the whirring of the panel being lowered.
'We're home.' Donny's voice was high-pitched and
triumphant. An instant later the side door of the van
rumbled open. Kay cringed as Donny bent over her.
His breath was rapid and warm on her cheek as he
released the gag. 'Kay, I don't want you to scream.
There's no one for miles around to hear you and you'll
only make me very nervous. Promise.'

She gulped in the cool air. Her tongue felt thick and
parched. 'Promise,' she whispered. He removed the
shackles and rubbed her ankles solicitously. The handcuffs were unsnapped from her wrists. He put an arm
around her and lifted her from the cot. Her legs were
numb. She stumbled and he half-carried her down the
high step to the ground.

The place where he had taken her was a shabby
frame house in a small clearing. A sagging porch held
a rusty swing. The windows were shuttered. The thick
trees around the clearing almost blotted out the last
slanting rays of the sun. Donny steered her towards the
house, unlocked the door, pushed her inside and snapped on the overhead light.

The room they were in was small and grimy. An
upright piano had long ago been painted white, but
peeling patches showed the original black finish. Several keys were missing. An overstuffed velour couch
and a chair must have at one time been bright red. Now
they were faded into shades of purple and orange. A
stained hooked rug covered the centre of the uneven
floor. A bottle of champagne in a plastic ice bucket
and two glasses were laid out on a metal table. Next
to the couch a crudely made bookcase was stuffed with
student notebooks.

'Look,' Donny said. He turned Kay around so she
was facing the wall opposite the piano. It was covered
with a poster-sized picture of her sitting with Donny at

sensed: perceived intuitively

whirring: vibrating sound ▶ **panel**: flat piece of glass, wood...
▶ **lowered**: made lower; low≠high ▶ **high-pitched**≠deep

rumbled... (with long low sounds) ▶ **cringed**: moved back in fear
breath: respiration ▶ **cheek**: side of face below eye
released: took away
no one: nobody

gulped in: took in (quickly) ▶ **thick**: heavy, solid, stiff
parched: very dry ▶ **removed**: took away, 'released'
rubbed: massaged ▶ **solicitously**: with solicitude
unsnapped: taken away quickly
lifted: picked up, raised
numb: without feeling ▶ **stumbled** (almost falling)
step (on which to walk out of the van to the ground)
shabby: old and in bad condition
frame... (made of wood) ▶ **clearing** (without trees) ▶ **sagging**
(inclined) ▶ **porch** (Am): veranda ▶ **rusty**: *rouillé* ▶ **swing** (for
children) ▶ **shuttered**; shutters (to cover windows at night)
▶ **blotted out**: hid ▶ **slanting**: oblique ▶ **steered**: took her to
unlocked: opened (with a key) ▶ **snapped on**: suddenly switched
on
the room **in** which they were ▶ **grimy**: very dirty
upright piano≠grand piano
peeling patches: places where the paint came off ▶ **finish**: final
coat of paint ▶ black and white **keys** ▶ **overstuffed**: with too
much material in it ▶ **couch**: sofa ▶ **bright** (≠dark) **red**
fade(d): lose colour ▶ **shade(s)**: nuance
stained≠clean ▶ **hooked rug**: made by hooking (*au crochet*)
▶ **uneven**: unequally flat, irregular
laid out: placed
crude(ly): rudimentary ▶ **stuffed with**: absolutely full of
student notebook(s): exercise book
so (Am): so that
was facing: was in front of
poster-sized: the size (dimension) of a poster

the prom. From the ceiling a crudely printed banner hung motionless. It read, 'Welcome home, Kay.'

Detective Jimmy Barrott was assigned to follow up the call from Michael Crandell, the guy who had reported his wife missing. On the way to the Garden View Motel he stopped at a fast-food place and ordered a hamburger and coffee.

He ate as he drove and by the time he got to the motel, his slight headache had disappeared and he was his usual cynical self. After twenty-five years in the prosecutor's office he felt he had seen it all.

Jimmy Barrott's instinct told him that this was a waste of time. A thirty-two-year-old woman goes to a reunion and doesn't get home right on the button. And the husband panics. Jimmy Barrott knew all about getting home late and not phoning. That was the primary reason he'd been divorced twice.

When the door to room 210 was opened, Jimmy had to admit that the young fellow, Michael Crandell, looked sick with worry. Nice-looking guy, Jimmy Barrott thought. About six feet one. The kind of rugged looks the girls go for. But Mike's first question got Jimmy's goat. 'What kept you so long?'

Jimmy settled himself in a chair at the table and opened his notebook. 'Listen,' he said, 'your wife is a couple of hours late getting back here. She's not officially missing for at least twenty-four hours. Did you two have a fight?'

He did not miss the guilty expression on Mike's face. 'You had a fight,' he pressed. 'Why don't you tell me about it and then let's figure where she'd go to cool off.'

To Mike's ears, he was telling it badly. Kay had been upset when they talked on the phone last night. She'd hung up on him. But it wasn't the way it seemed. Quickly he sketched their background. Kay had taught at Garden State High for two years. They'd met in Chicago at her sister's and been married from there.

ceiling (top of room) ▶ **banner**: long piece of cloth (like a flag)
motionless: not moving, still ▶ **it read**: one could read on it

assigned: given as a job ▶ **follow up**: do sth as a result of
(telephone) **call** ▶ **guy**: (Am) fellow, man
on the way to: as he went to
place: shop, restaurant... ▶ **order(ed)**: ask for

by the time: when ▶ **he got to**: he arrived at
slight≠bad, severe ▶ a **headache** is less severe than a migraine

prosecutor (in a criminal court) ▶ **he had seen it all**: he knew
all about his job, he knew all the ropes ▶ **a waste of time** ; to
waste or to lose time
right on the button (Am, fam): at exactly the right time
panics; to panic, to get panicky
primary: main, principal
once, **twice** (also two times), three times, four times...
the door **to** room: notice the preposition!

sick with worry: terribly worried
six feet one (inch); foot: 30.48 cm; inch: 2.54 cm ▶ **rugged**
looks: manly, virile appearance ▶ **go for**: are attracted to
got... goat: irritated him ▶ **...long?**: why didn't you come earlier?
settled...: sat comfortably
notebook: small book for writing notes ▶ **a couple of**: two or
more, a few
at least≠at most
fight: quarrel
he did not miss: he did not fail to see ▶ **guilty**: culpable
he pressed (insisting)
figure: try to find out
cool off: become calmer, calm down
badly: in the wrong way
upset: distressed, unhappy ▶ **on** the phone

sketched: gave a short description of ▶ **background**: social
milieu, family, education... ▶ **met** (for the first time)
at her sister's (house)

He'd never known her New Jersey friends. There was
no point calling her sister. Jean and her husband and
kids were in Europe on vacation.

'Give me a description of the car,' Jimmy Barrott
ordered. White 1986 Toyota. Arizona license plate. He
scribbled the numbers. 'Pretty far to drive,' he
observed.

'I had vacation coming. We decided to wind it
around the company meeting and the alumni reunion.
We're supposed to start driving back to Arizona
tomorrow.'

Jimmy closed his notebook. 'My hunch is she's
having dinner and a drink by herself or with some old
friends and will be back in the next couple of hours.'
He glanced at the framed pictures on the table. 'One
of those your wife?'

'That one.' He'd snapped the picture in front of the
condo. It had been a hot day. Kay was wearing shorts
and a T-shirt. Her hair was held back by a band. She
looked about sixteen. With the T-shirt clinging to her
breasts and her long, slender legs in open sandals, she
also looked damned sexy. Mike sensed that that was
the reaction this detective had.

'Why don't you let me have this picture?' Jimmy
Barrott suggested. Deftly he slipped it from the frame.
'If she isn't home in the next twenty-four hours, we'll
make up a missing person's report.'

Some instinct made Jimmy Barrott walk around the
parking lot before he went to his own car. By now the
lot was almost full. There were a couple of white
Toyotas in it but none with Arizona plates. Then one
car at the end of the lot, off by itself, caught his eye.
He sauntered over to it.

Five minutes later he was rapping sharply at the door
of room 210. 'Your car is in the parking lot,' he told
Mike. 'The keys were on the floor. Looks as though
your wife left them for you.'

As he studied the incredulous look on Mike's face,
the telephone rang. Both men rushed to answer it.

New Jersey is a state in the East ▶ **there was no point (**in**)...**:
it was useless to... ▶ **Jean**, Jane
on vacation (Am): on holiday

order(ed): command ▶ **license** (metal) **plate**
scribbled: wrote quickly, badly ▶ **pretty**: quite, rather
observed: remarked, said
wind it...: combine vacation, company meeting and alumni
reunion
driving back: going back by car

closed: shut ▶ **my hunch is** (that): my intuition is telling me that

next: following
framed picture(s): photograph in a frame (made of silver)
(is) **one of those** (pictures of) **your wife?**
snapped: taken (rapidly**)** ; take a snapshot of

held back: kept in place; hold, held, held
clinging: pressed against
a woman with a baby at the **breast(s)** (drinking milk) ▶ **slender**: thin
and attractive ▶ **damned** (fam): very ▶ **sensed**: felt (vaguely,
intuitively)

deftly: dexterously ▶ **slipped...**: took away from, quickly
if she isn't (at) **home**
a missing person's report (saying Kay has disappeared)

his **own** car (not anybody else's) ('own' is emphatic)
full≠empty ▶ **a couple of**: two (or a few)
none: not one of them
off by itself: isolated ▶ **caught...**: drew his attention
sauntered: walked slowly, nonchalantly
rapping sharply: knocking with energy, suddenly, quickly
tell, **told**, told; tell sb sth; say sth <u>to</u> sb
the floor (of the car) ▶ (it) **looks as though** (as if)

look: appearance, aspect
ring, **rang**, rung ▶ **both men**: both Mike and Jimmy Barrott

Jimmy Barrott reached it first, picked up the receiver and held it so that he could hear what was said.

Mike's 'hello' was almost inaudible. And then the men listened as Kay said, 'Mike, I'm sorry to do this to you but I need time to think. I left the car in the lot. Go back to Arizona. It's all over for us. I'll be in touch with you about a divorce.'

'No... Kay... please... I won't leave without you.'

There was a click. Jimmy Barrott felt reluctant sympathy for the shocked and bewildered young man. He took Kay's picture and laid it on the table. 'That's just the way my second wife took off,' he told Mike. 'The only difference is while I was at work she had the movers in. Left me with a beer mug and my laundry.'

The remark cut through the numbness. 'But that's it,' Mike said. 'Don't you see?' He pointed to the dresser. 'Kay's toilet articles. She wouldn't leave without them. Her makeup is in the bathroom cabinet. The book she was reading.' He opened the closet door. 'Her clothes. What woman doesn't bring anything personal with her?'

'You'd be surprised how many,' Jimmy Barrott told him. 'I'm sorry, Mr Crandell, but I have to write this up as a domestic affair.'

He went back to the office to file his report, then drove home. But even when he'd gone to bed, Jimmy Barrott couldn't sleep. The neatly hung clothes, the toilet articles so carefully laid out. Something in his gut was telling him Kay Crandell would have taken them with her. But she'd phoned.

Had she?

Jimmy sat bolt upright. Some woman phoned. He had only Mike Crandell's word that it was his wife's voice. And Mike Crandell and his wife had had a fight just before she disappeared.

Hours passed as Mike sat by the phone. She'll call again, he told himself. She'll change her mind. She'll come back.

reached: came to ▶ **picked up** (took up) the (telephone) **receiver** ▶ say, **said,** said

think, thought, thought: reflect; think hard **over**: finished ▶ **I'll be in touch with you**: I'll conctact you

leave, left, left: go away (to Arizona)
reluctant: unwilling; reluctantly, without enthusiasm
bewildered: perplexed, puzzled, confused
lay, **laid**, laid: put, placed (≠lie, lay, lain)
the way (in which)... ▶ **took off**: went away (leaving me)
at work: working (notice the preposition)
movers take away furniture... ▶ **mug** (for beer, hot drinks)
cut through... (and put an end to it) ▶ **numbness**: torpor
pointed to: showed with his finger
she wouldn't leave: it wouldn't be like her to leave
makeup: powder, cream... ▶ **cabinet**: cupboard

how many (women go away without bringing anything personal)
write up: write a report
domestic: concerning family relationship and life at home

file: officially record (keeping it for reference) ▶ **drove home**: no preposition!
neatly: very carefully
something in his gut...: instinctively he felt sure that...

had she? (really phoned herself)
bolt upright: very straight ▶ **some woman** (or other) ▶ **he had...**
word: only Mike Crandell had told him
fight: quarrel, row, argument

by: next to, near
change her mind: change her decision

Would she?

At last Mike got up. He stripped and fell onto the bed, the side nearest the phone, ready to grasp the receiver at the first ring. Then he closed his eyes and began to cry.

Kay bit her lip, trying not to scream in protest as Donny broke the phone connection. Donny was smiling at her solicitously. 'That was very good, Kay.'

Would he have carried out his threat? He'd warned her that if she did not say exactly what he'd written and say it convincingly, he would go to the motel tonight and kill Mike. 'I was in your room twice this past week, you know,' he told her. 'I do odd jobs at the motel. It was easy to make a key.' Then he had led her into the bedroom. The furniture here consisted of a sagging double bed covered with a cheap chenille spread, a card-table nightstand and a battered dresser. 'Do you like the bedspread?' Donny asked. 'I told the woman it was a present for my wife. She said most women like white chenille.' He pointed to the comb and brush and mirror on top of the dresser. 'They're almost exactly the same colour as yours.' He opened the closet. 'Do you like your new clothes? They're all size eight just like the ones you had in the motel.' There were a couple of cotton skirts and T-shirts, a raincoat, a robe, a flowered print dress. 'There's some underwear and a nightgown in the drawers,' Donny told her proudly. 'And look, the shoes are your size too, 7 medium. I got you sneakers and loafers and heels. I want my wife to be well dressed.'

'Donny, I can't be your wife,' she'd whispered.

He'd looked puzzled. 'But you're going to be. You always wanted to marry me.' It was then she'd noticed the chain neatly folded in the corner by the bed and attached to a metal plate on the wall. Donny had seen her horrified expression. 'Don't worry, Kay. I have one in every room. It's just that at night I'll be sleeping in the living room and I don't want you to try to leave

would she? (come back)
at last: finally ▶ **got up**: stood up ▶ **stripped**: took off his clothes
side (of bed) ▶ **grasp**: seize, take and hold firmly
at the first ring: the first time it rang; ring, rang, rung
to cry: to weep, wept, wept

scream: give a loud, sharp cry ▶ **in protest**: to protest
break, **broke**, broken ▶ (telephone) **connection**
... very good (the way you said what I wanted you to say)
carried out his threat: acted according to his menace

convincingly; to convince
kill: put to death
odd jobs: many different small pieces of work
led her into: taken her into; lead, led, led
furniture; a bed (a couch, a chair...) is a piece of furniture
sag(ging): curve down in the middle ▶ **cheap**: poor quality
card-table used as a **nightstand** (Am), night table ▶ **battered**:
old and in bad condition
a present: a gift (give, gave, given)

top≠bottom ▶ **they're the same colour**: don't use 'of'!

size (Large, Extra Large...); **8**=38; **7 medium**=39 (shoes)
skirts: unlike a dress, a skirt covers only part of the body
robe (worn after a bath) ▶ **flowered**: with flowers printed...
nightgown: nightdress ▶ **drawer(s)**: container that can be pulled
out ▶ **proudly**; pride, high opinion of oneself
got (bought) **you** ▶ **loafer(s)**: flat shoe without laces
heels: women's shoes that are very high at the back
whispered: said very softly, very quietly
puzzled: intrigued ▶ **you're going to be** (my wife)
marry me (no preposition!); be married to sb
neatly: impeccably ▶ **folded** (so that one part covers another),
put away ▶ **metal plate**: flat piece of metal

at night (notice the preposition!): during the night
I don't want you to try: infinitive clause

me. And during the day I have to go to work so I have it fixed that you'll be comfortable in the living room.'

He'd taken her back to the living room and ceremoniously uncorked the champagne. 'To us.'

Now as Kay watched him put the receiver in place, her mouth felt sour remembering the taste of the warm, sugary champagne, the greasy hamburgers Donny had cooked.

All through the meal he'd said nothing. Then he'd told her to finish her coffee, that he'd be right back. When he returned he was clean-shaven. 'I only grew the beard so people wouldn't recognize me at the school,' he said proudly.

After that he made her finish the champagne with him and call Mike. Now he sighed. 'Kay, you must be tired. I'll let you go to bed soon. But first I'd like to read you a couple of chapters of my first book about you.' With almost a swagger, he walked over to the bookcase and took out one of the notebooks.

This isn't real, Kay thought.

But this was real. Donny settled himself in the over-stuffed chair opposite her. The room was chilly now but sweat glistened on his face and arms and stained his polo shirt. His unnaturally pale skin was accentuated by dark circles under his eyes. When he'd taken off his sunglasses, she'd been surprised to see how blue his eyes were. She'd remembered them as being brown. They *are* brown, she told herself. He must be wearing coloured contacts. Everything about him is fantasy, she thought. He looked up at her almost shyly. 'I feel like I'm a kid back in school,' he said.

A tiny whisper of hope told Kay that she might be able to establish some authority over him, teacher to student. But when he began to read, her throat closed in near-panic. 'June Third. Last night I went to the prom with Kay,' he intoned. 'We danced every dance. When I drove her home, she cried in my arms. She said her family was forcing her to marry a man she did not love and that she wanted me to come for her when

so: in consequence, consequently, therefore
I have it fixed (so) **that you'll be comfortable**
he had taken (led, steered) **her back to...**
uncorked: opened (removed the cork from the bottle)

sour: bitter, acid ▶ **the taste**; to taste (nice...)
sugary: tasting of sugar ▶ **greasy**: (too) fat
cooked; to cook a meal; a cook is a person
all through the meal (from beginning to end)
right back: back immediately, in no time
clean-shaven: clean, completely; shave, cut hair, beard with a
razor ▶ **'so'** is very often used in American for 'so that'

made her finish: forced her to finish
call (on the phone) ▶ **sighed**; sigh, prolonged deep audible respiration ▶ **soon**: before long

swagger: superior, insolent way of walking

this isn't real: this cannot be happening
settled himself: sat comfortably
chilly: uncomfortably cold
sweat: perspiration ▶ **glistened**: shone (shine, shone, shone)
▶ **stained**: left dirty marks (stains) on
taken off≠put on

told herself: thought to herself
contacts: contact lenses ▶ **everything about** (in) **him**
fantasy: imagination, imagining ▶ **shyly**: uneasily, timidly
I feel like... (as if I was a school boy again)
tiny: minuscule ▶ **whisper**: murmur ▶ **might** (perhaps)
some (sort of) **authority over him** (notice the preposition !)
throat: *gorge* ▶ **closed**, shut (no reflexive pronouns) ▶ **in near-
panic**: on the verge of panic
intoned: said in a slow, solemn voice
drove her home: took her home in my car
a man (whom) **she did not love**
come for her: come and take her away

I am able to take care of her. My beautiful Kay. I promise you that one day I shall claim you as my wife.'

A sleepless night and the fact that he had absolutely no coffee in his apartment made Jimmy Barrott unusually grumpy. After a stop for coffee, he headed for the office. When the prosecutor's office was cleared, Jimmy sauntered in.

'Something stinks,' he told his boss, 'about that domestic affair report I filed last night. I want permission to look into the husband.' Tersely he related the interview with Mike, the finding of the car, the telephone call.

The prosecutor listened and nodded. 'Start digging,' he said. 'Let me know if you want any help.'

At the first sign of dawn, Mike got up, shaved and showered. He hoped that the hot, then cold needles of water would wash away the sluggishness from his brain.

Somewhere during the dark hours of the night, his despair at Kay's disappearance had hardened into certainty that she would not have abandoned him that way. He pulled a notebook from his briefcase and between gulps of coffee began to jot down the possible actions he could take. Virginia Murphy O'Neil. She'd been with Kay right at the end of the picnic. She'd seen Kay leave. Maybe Kay had told her something that didn't seem important then. He'd go to Virginia's home and talk to her. Detective Barrott had spotted the car at ten o'clock. But no one knew what time it had been left there. He'd talk to the motel employees. Maybe someone had seen Kay alone or with someone.

He wanted to sit by the phone, to wait because Kay might call again, but that was crazy. Mike's blood chilled at the thought that maybe she wouldn't be able to call again.

His first stop was at the motel telephone operator's station. The operator assured him that she was much

take care of her: look after her
claim you as my wife: ask you to be my wife; claim, demand

sleepless night (when you cannot sleep at all)

grumpy: irritable ▶ **headed for**: went in the direction of
cleared (of the people in it), vacant, empty

stinks (fam): sth dishonest has been done; to stink of corruption
look into: try to find the truth about ▶ **tersely**: concisely
the finding: the fact that the car was found

nodded: moved his head down in approval ▶ **dig(ging)**: study very carefully

dawn: daybreak, first light of day ▶ **got up** (out of bed)
needle(s): small, thin, sharp-pointed piece of metal
wash away: eliminate ▶ **sluggishness**: slowness, lethargy
brain: the centre of thought in our heads
dark: unhappy or without hope
hardened: become hard or harder (figuratively)

briefcase: case used for carrying papers or documents
jot down: make a quick note of ▶ **the... actions he could take**: what he could possibly do
right at the end: at the very end; right, exactly

spotted: noticed, taken notice of
(at) **what time it had been left there**
employee(s): employed by an employer; employment

wait (without an object) but wait <u>for</u> sb, wait <u>for</u> sth
crazy: mad ▶ red **blood** in the veins ▶ **chilled** (with horror)
thought: idea

too busy to give messages to people who called in but she was very happy to take any that he might receive. He made his voice confidential. 'Look, you ever had a fight with your boyfriend?'

She laughed. 'Like every night.'

'Last night I had a row with my wife. She walked out on me. I have to go out now, but I'm pretty sure she'll call. Please, can you plug the line or something so you won't forget to give her this message?'

The operator's heavily painted eyes sparkled with curiosity. She read the note aloud. In block letters Mike had written, 'If Kay Crandell phones, tell her Mike has to talk to her. He'll go along with anything she wants but please leave a phone number or time when she'll call back.'

The operator's look was filled now with sympathy and a certain coyness. 'I don't know why any woman would be dope enough to walk out on you,' she told him.

Mike slipped a twenty-dollar bill in her hand. 'I'm counting on you to play Cupid.'

Talking to employees who might have seen the white Toyota come into the parking lot was hopeless. There was no parking-lot attendant. The one security guard had been inside the motel most of the evening. 'Just started today,' he told Mike. 'Otherwise I wouldn't be here either. Nope. Not a wink of trouble.' He scratched his head. 'Come to think of it, they did have one car grabbed last year but it was abandoned two miles away. The owner said even a crook could tell it was a lemon.' He chuckled.

Two hours later, Mike was thirty miles away sitting across the table in Virginia O'Neil's house. She was a small, trim young woman who had been in Kay's choir the last year Kay taught at Garden State High. The kitchen was large and cheerful and opened into an airy recreation room cluttered with toys. Virginia's two-year-old twins were playing there with noisy, unrestrained energy.

called in: phoned the motel operator's station
take any (message)
look: listen ▶ **you ever had?**: did you ever have?

like... (Am): everynight, to be frank
row: quarrel ▶ **walk(ed) out on**: leave one's husband or wife
suddenly ▶ **pretty** (adv): quite
plug: connect ▶ **the** (telephone) **line**

heavily painted (with a lot of mascara) ▶ **sparkled**: shone in
small bright flashes ▶ **block letters** : block capitals (as in printing)

go along with: agree with, accept

call back: return a telephone call (to me)
filled with, full <u>of</u>: notice the prepositions!
coyness; coy, pretending to be shy (timid) in flirtation
dope (fam): stupid person, fool

slipped: put quietly, secretly ▶ **bill** (Am): banknote
play Cupid; try to arrange for two people to fall in love with each
other; Cupid is the Roman god of love
hopeless: without hope≠hopeful
attendant: man in charge ▶ **the one**: the only one ▶ **security
guard** (in charge of security in the car park)
(I) **just started** (working) ▶ **otherwise**: if not
nope (fam): no ▶ **not a wink...**: not the smallest incident
scratched (with his fingernails) ▶ **come...** (suddenly
realizing sth) ▶ **grabbed** (sl): stolen, robbed
owner: proprietor ▶ **crook** (fam): dishonest person
tell: see, realize ▶ **lemon** (fam): useless car ▶ **chuckled**:
laughed; a chuckle: a suppressed laugh

trim: neat and attractive
teach**, taught,** taught; the teaching profession
cheerful: pleasant, bright ▶ **airy**: bright and spacious
recreation room (for relaxation, games) ▶ **cluttered**: filled
▶ **toys** (to play with) ▶ **twins** (born on the same day) ▶ **unrestrained**: extreme, intense, uncontrolled

Mike did not attempt to concoct a story about why he was looking for Kay. He liked Virginia and instinctively trusted her. By the time he had finished, he saw his own sick worry mirrored in Virginia's eyes. 'That is *weird*,' she told him. 'Kay wouldn't pull that kind of stunt. She's just too considerate.'

'How much of her did you see at the reunion?'

A teddy bear went flying past Mike's foot. An instant later a small figure hurtled by him and tackled it.

'At ease, Kevin,' Virginia ordered. She explained to Mike, 'My aunt gave the kids teddy bears yesterday. Dina is cuddling hers. Kevin is tackling his.'

This is what Kay wanted, Mike thought. A house like this, a couple of kids. The thought gave him a new and disquieting possibility. 'Did most people bring their children to the reunion?'

'Oh, there were loads of kids around.' Virginia's face became contemplative. 'You know, Kay did look a little wistful when she was holding Dina the other day and she said, "All my students have families. I never expected it would turn out like this for me." '

Mike rose to leave a few minutes later. 'What are you going to do?' Virginia asked. He took Kay's picture from his pocket. 'I'm going to get posters made and just hand them out. It's the only thing I can think of.'

When Donny finally decided it was time to go to bed, he told Kay to change in the tiny bathroom. It held a small sink, a commode and a makeshift shower. He handed her the nightgown he'd bought, a low-cut, transparent scrap of nylon edged with imitation lace. The robe matched. As she changed, Kay frantically tried to decide how to deal with him if he tried to attack her. He could certainly overpower her. Her only hope was to try to take charge, to establish a teacher-student relationship.

But when she emerged he didn't attempt to touch her. 'Get into bed, Kay,' he said. He turned down the

attempt: try ▶ **story**: invented story
looking for: trying to find
trusted her: believed that she was honest
sick worry: extreme worry ▶ **mirrored**: reflected
weird: bizarre ▶ **pull a stunt**: do sth silly or risky
just: simply ▶ **considerate**: careful not to trouble others
how much of her...?: how long did you see her?
teddy bear (to play with) ▶ **went flying past** (like a plane)
figure: shape of a person ▶ **hurtled**: moved very fast
▶ **tackled**: forced it to the floor ▶ **at ease**: calm down
aunt(s) and uncles
cuddling: holding as a way of showing love or affection

disquieting: alarming, worrying

loads of (fam): plenty of, lots of
contemplative: showing careful thought ▶ **did look**: seemed in
fact ▶ **wistful**: sad and thoughtful
families; a family of four (four children)
turn out like this: happen like this
rose: stood up; rise, rose, risen ▶ **leave**, take his leave, go

get (or have) **posters** (enlarged photos here) **made** (by sb)
hand them out (here and there): distribute, 'deliver' ▶ **I can think
of**: of which I can think

change: no reflexive pronoun! ▶ **tiny**: very small
sink (Am): washbasin ▶ **commode**: toilets ▶ **makeshift**: used as
an improvised substitute ▶ **low-cut** (showing neck and top of
chest) ▶ **scrap**: small piece ▶ **edged**; edge, border ▶ **lace**: fine
cloth ▶ **matched**: corresponded in colour ▶ **frantically**: desperately ▶ **deal with**: act, behave
overpower her: defeat her (being stronger than she is)
take charge (of): take control of (a situation)

emerged (out of the bathroom) ▶ **attempt**, make an attempt
turned down (in a downward or backward position)

spread. There were blue-flowered muslin sheets and pillowcases on the bed. They looked stiff and new. She walked firmly to the bed. 'I'm very tired, Donny,' she said crisply. 'I want to get to sleep.'

'Oh, Kay, I promise you, I won't touch you till we're married.' He covered her, then said, 'I'm sorry, Kay, but I can't take a chance that you'll try to get away while I'm asleep.' And then he shackled her foot to the chain.

All night she'd lain awake, trying to pray, trying to plan, only able to whisper *Mike, help me, Mike, find me.* Towards dawn she fell into an uneasy sleep. She awakened to find Donny staring at her. Even in the semidark, there was no mistaking the urgency in his stance. Through clenched teeth, he whispered, 'I just wanted to make sure you were comfortable, Kay. You look so pretty when you're asleep. I can hardly wait till we're married.'

He wanted her to cook breakfast for him. 'Your future husband has a good appetite, Kay.' At eight-thirty, he settled her in the living room. 'I'm sorry to close the shutters again but I can't risk having someone walk by and look in. Not that it ever happens, but you'll understand.' He shackled her leg to the chain in the living room. 'I measured it,' he told her. 'You can get into the bathroom. I'm leaving stuff for sandwiches and a pitcher of water and some sodas right here on the table. You can reach the piano. I want you to prac-tise. And if you want to read, you can read all my books. They're all about you, Kay. I've been writing about you for these whole eight years.'

He left the recorder-phone in the padlocked wire cage near the ceiling. 'I'll leave the conference call on, Kay. You'll hear people phoning jobs in for me. I beep my messages from the phone in the van every hour or so. I'll talk to you then but you won't be able to talk to me. I'm sorry. It's a real busy day, so I may not get back till six or seven.' As he left, he lifted her chin in his hand. 'Miss me, won't you, sweetheart?'

(bed)spread ▶ (white...) **sheets** (to make a bed with)
pillowcase(s); pillow(s): cushion for one's head ▶ **stiff**≠soft

crisply: in a decisive tone

covered (with the sheet)
take a chance: take the risk
asleep: sleeping ▶ **shackled**: attached, fastened

awake≠asleep ▶ **pray**: ask God to help her

towards: just before ▶ **uneasy**≠comfortable, relaxed
awakened: stopped sleeping ▶ **staring**: looking fixedly
there was no mistaking: she was certain about ▶ **urgency**:
pressure ▶ **stance**: attitude ▶ **clenched**: held firmly together
make sure: see for certain
pretty: attractive ▶ **hardly**: only just, barely

cook breakfast: get breakfast ready
has a good appetite: notice the use of the article!
settle(d): put in a comfortable position
close: shut, shut, shut ▶ **shutters**: to cover windows at night
not that it ever happens: it never happens in fact
shackled: put shackles (metal rings) on
I measured it (the chain)
stuff (fam): things (here bread, butter...)
pitcher: container for holding liquids
reach: get as far as ▶ **practise**: play regularly

these whole (entire, complete) **eight years** (an emphatic way of
saying it) ▶ **recorder-phone** (for messages) ▶ **padlocked**: attached ▶ **wire** (metal) ▶ **ceiling** (top of room) ▶ **conference call**
(to hear messages) ▶ **beep**: listen to
every hour or so: approximately every hour

a real busy day (Am): a really busy day (with a lot of work)
lifted: raised ▶ **chin**: part of the face under the mouth
(you'll) **miss me** (regret my absence) ▶ **sweatheart**: darling

His kiss on her cheek was prim. His arm around her waist tightened convulsively.

He had bolted the shutters before he left and the dim overhead light cast shadows throughout the room. She stood on the couch, straining the chain until the shackles ripped her ankle, but it was impossible to get at the wire cage and, even so, it was padlocked. There was no chance of making a phone call.

The chain was attached to a metal plate on the wall. There were four screws holding the plate in place. If she could somehow undo those screws, she could get out. How near was it to the highway? How fast could she move with the shackle on her ankle and carrying the chain? What could she use to undo the screws?

Feverishly, Kay searched the living room. The plastic knife he'd left snapped when she tried to twist it into the head of a screw. Frustrated tears filled her eyes. She pulled the cushions from the couch. The upholstery was ripped and she could see the wires but there was no way she could break one loose.

She dragged herself over to the piano. If she could reach into the strings maybe there was something sharp she could pull loose.

There wasn't.

There was no way to loosen the metal plate. Her only hope would be if someone happened to come by while he was away. But who? There was some mail on top of the bookcase. Most of it was addressed to a box number in Howville. A few pieces had the address of this place, 4 Timber Lane, Howville. Each of them had the box number pencilled on the enveloppe, so Donny did not have postal delivery.

Her eye fell on the rows of black-and-white student notebooks. He had told her to read them. She pulled out a half dozen of them and dragged herself over to the couch. The light was dim and she frowned in concentration. She'd put on the dress she'd been wearing yesterday at the picnic, wanting to keep some sense of her own identity. But the dress was wrinkled now

prim: prudish, formal

waist: *taille* ▶ **tightened**: became tight, firm

bolted: locked with a metal bar ▶ **dim**: not bright

cast shadows throughout...: caused darkness in places in the whole room ▶ **straining**: pulling beyond limit

ripped: tore, cut sharply ▶ **get at**: get as far as

even so: even if she did get at the wire cage

making a phone call: calling, ringing up, giving a buzz...

attached: fastened

screw(s) (driven into the wall with a 'screwdriver')

somehow: in one way or another ▶ **undo**: unfasten

highway (Am): main road connecting towns and cities ▶ **fast**: rapidly

feverishly: frantically ▶ **searched** (trying to find sth)

snapped: broke with a sudden sharp noise ▶ **twist**: turn

tear(s) (rolling down her cheeks as she cried)

cushion(s) (to make a couch more comfortable)

upholstery: covering material ▶ **wire(s)**: metal spring

way: method ▶ **break loose** (≠fasten): pull out, tear off

dragged herself: moved with difficulty

strings produce sound ▶ **sharp**: pointed

pull loose: detach

there wasn't (anything sharp)

to loosen: to make loose (≠tight, firmly fixed), to free

happened to come by: passed by, arrived by chance

mail (Am): post (letters, postcards...)

box number: address at the post office ▶ **pieces** (of mail)

pencilled: written with a pencil

did not have... delivery: no mail brought home to him

row(s): line of notebooks... next to each other

read, read, read (with different pronunciations!)

a half dozen or half a dozen (six)

frowned: drew her eyebrows together (causing lines on forehead) ▶ **put on**≠taken off (clothes)

wrinkled; wrinkle: line or fold on cloth made by pressing it

and she felt soiled. Soiled by her presence in this place, by the memory of his hands convulsively gripping her waist, by her sense of being a caged animal with a berserk keeper. The thought brought near-hysteria. Get a grip on yourself, she said aloud. Mike is trying to find you. He will find you. It was as though she could feel the intensity of his love. Mike. Mike. I love you. She didn't want to move around anymore. She wanted to stay in one place. Even Donny Rubel had known that. And he was granting that wish. Kay realized she was laughing aloud, a shrieking sobbing laugh that ended in a frenzy of tears.

But at least it brought a certain release. After a few minutes, she dried her face with the back of her hand and began to read.

The books were all alike. A day-by-day odyssey of a fantasy life starting with that night at the prom. Some of the entries were written as future plans. 'When Kay and I are together, we will take a camping trip to Colorado. We will live in a tent and share the rustic, outdoor life of our forefathers. We will have a double sleeping bag and she will lie in my arms because she is a little afraid of the sounds of the animals. I will protect her and comfort her.' Other times he wrote as though they had been together. 'Kay and I had a wonderful day. We went into New York to the South Street Seaport. I bought her a new blouse and blue high-heeled shoes. Kay likes to hold my hand when we are walking. She loves me very much and never wants to be away from me. We have decided that if one or the other ever gets sick, we will not risk being separated. We are not afraid to die together. We will be in heaven for all eternity. We are lovers.'

At times it was almost impossible to make out the nearly illegible scrawl. Kay ignored her growing headache as she read book after book. The depths of Donny's madness brought her to the edge of panic. She must finish reading every one of the books. Somehow, some way, she might get a clue as to how she could

soiled: made dirty (psychologically), less respectful
gripping: taking and keeping a firm hold of
caged: kept in a cage (by a 'keeper')
berserk: crazy and out of control ▶ **get a grip on yourself**: start controlling your emotions

feel, felt, felt

one and the same place ('one' is emphatic here)
granting...: giving her what she wanted
shrieking: piercing ▶ **sobbing** (convulsively catching her breath)
frenzy of tears: uncontrolled crying or weeping
release (of tension...), feeling of comfort after pain, worry
dried; to dry, to make dry (≠wet) ▶ **back** (of hand)≠palm
begin, **began**, begun
alike: the same
a fantasy life (in which every event is imagined, unreal)
entries; entry (in a dictionary...)
take a camping trip: go camping; trip: journey (travel)
share: live (here) ▶ **rustic**: simple ▶ **outdoor**: in the open air
forefathers: ancestors ▶ **double**≠single

comfort: to comfort, to bring help, kindness, consolation
Kay and I: notice the personal pronoun 'I' (subject)
South Street Seaport (in Manhattan)
blouse (at the top) and skirt ▶ **high-heeled**: with high heels
to hold, held, held
she loves me very much: don't separate verb and object!

gets sick: falls ill
heaven: paradise
we are lovers: we love each other
at times: sometimes ▶ **make out**: see clearly, read (here)
scrawl: careless writing ▶ **growing**: getting worse
depth(s); deep, profound
the edge of panic: 'near-panic'; edge: limit, border
somehow, some way: in one way or another
clue: sign, indication ▶ **as to how**: concerning the way

persuade him to release her, to take her somewhere in public. He constantly wrote about sharing outings with her.

From about ten o'clock on, the phone began to ring. She could hear the messages that were left for Donny. Every nerve in her body vibrated at the sound of the impersonal voices. *Listen to me, she wanted to shriek. Help me.*

Donny apparently had an active repair service. A pizza parlour call–could he get over as soon as possible? One of the ovens wasn't working. Several housewives–could he take a look at the television? The VCR? A window-pane was broken. Every hour or so, Donny beeped in for messages, then left a message for her. 'Kay, darling, I miss you very much. Do you see how busy I am? I've already made two hundred dollars this morning. I'll be able to take very good care of you.'

After each call, she went back to reading. Over and over, in all the books, Donny kept referring to his mother. 'When she was eighteen she let my father go too far and she got pregnant with me and had to get married. My father walked out on her when I was a baby and he blamed her for everything. I will never be like my father. I will not put a finger on Kay until we are married. Otherwise she might grow to hate me too and dislike our children.'

In the next to last book she learned his plans. 'On television I heard a preacher say that marriages have the best chance when people have known each other for four seasons. That there is something in the human spirit just as there is in nature that needs that cycle. I was in Kay's class in the fall and winter. I will take her away during the reunion. It will still be spring. We will exchange our vows together with only God as our witness on the first day of summer. That will be on Sunday, 21 June. We will then leave and tour the country together, the two of us, lovers.'

Today was Thursday, 18 June.

release (a prisoner...): set free
sharing outings...: going out with her; outing: short pleasure trip

from about ten o'clock on (continuing from then)

to shriek: to make a very high, loud sound (a shriek)

repair service: 'fix-it business' (p 14)
pizza parlour (Am): pizzeria ▶ **get over**: come over
oven(s) (to cook food in) ▶ **working**: operating successfully

Video **C**assette **R**ecorder, to record or watch films ▶ **window-
pane** (made of glass) ▶ **beeped in for...** (to see if he had any
message) ▶ **I miss you**: notice the construction
made (earned)**...** dollars; make money (not 'do'!)

went back to reading: started reading again ▶ **over and over**:
repeatedly, constantly ▶ **kept...**: always referred

be pregnant: expect a baby; got pregnant <u>with</u> me
walked out on her: left her, let her down
blamed her <u>for</u> everything; put or lay the blame on sb
put a finger on: touch
grow to hate me: gradually start to hate (detest) me
dislike≠like
next to last: last but one (not the very last one)
preacher (Am): clergyman; to preach (in church)
the best chance (of success)

needs: requires
fall (Am): autumn ▶ **take her away** (forcefully), 'abduct'

vow(s): marriage vows; a vow: a serious, solemn promise
witness: sb who sees what happens (an accident...)
tour the country: visit the country (on a tour)
the two of us: notice the way this is said

At four o'clock a call came in from the Garden View Motel. Could Donny stop by this afternoon? A couple of television sets weren't working.

The Garden View Motel. Room 210. Mike.

Donny phoned a few minutes later. His voice had an echoing, hollow sound. 'See what I mean, Kay. I do a lot of work over at the motel. I'm glad they called. It will give me a chance to see if Mike Crandell is going to clear out. I hope you've been practising our songs. I really want to sing with you tonight. Goodbye for now, my darling.'

There was anger in his voice when he said Mike's name. He's afraid, Kay thought. If anything upsets his plans, he'll go crazy. She must not antagonize him. She put the books back in the shelves and dragged herself over to the piano. It was hopelessly out of tune. The missing keys meant that everything she attempted to play was riddled with discordant sounds.

When Donny came in, it was nearly eight o'clock. His face was set in grim, angry lines. 'Crandell isn't going home,' he told Kay. 'He's asking a lot of questions about you. He's passing out your picture.'

Mike was at the motel. Mike had known there was something wrong. Oh, Mike, Kay thought. Find me. I'll go anywhere, anyplace. I'll have a baby in Kalamazoo or Peoria. What does it matter where we live as long as we're together?

It was as though Donny could read her thoughts. He stood in the doorway glowering at her. 'You didn't make him believe you when you talked to him last night. It's your fault, Kay.'

He started across the room towards her. She shrank back on the couch and the chain yanked the shackle on her ankle. A thin trickle of blood, warm and slippery, dripped from her bruised flesh.

Donny noticed. 'Oh, Kay, that hurt you, I can tell.' He went into the bathroom and returned with a warm, wet cloth. Tenderly he lifted her leg from the floor and laid it across his lap. 'It will feel much better now,' he

stop by: come and see
television set(s), radio set... ▶ **weren't working**: were out of order
phoned; to phone sb (no preposition!)
hollow: low (deep), dull (not clear) and echoing (resonating)
glad: happy
chance: opportunity
clear out (fam): leave ▶ **practising** (in order to sing better)

anger: rage; be angry with sb, at or about sth
upsets...: puts them out of order, causes them to go wrong
antagonize him: make him feel hostile towards her
put back: replaced ▶ **shelves**; shelf (for putting books on)
hopelessly: terribly ▶ **out of tune**≠producing the right notes
mean, **meant**, meant
riddled with: very full of

set: fixed into a firm expression ▶ **grim**: very serious, severe

passing out: handing out, giving out

wrong: not right
anyplace (Am): anywhere ▶ **Kalamazoo**, Michigan; **Peoria**, Arizona ▶**... matter...?**: where we live is of no importance **as long as** (if, on condition that) we are together.

doorway: space where door opens ▶ **glowering**: looking in an angry way ▶ **believe you**: think what you said was true
it's your fault: no preposition!
started (walking) **across** ▶ **shrank back**: moved backwards (out of fear)...▶ **yanked**: pulled suddenly, forcefully
trickle (flowing in small quantity) ▶ **slippery**: viscous
dripped: fell in small drops ▶ **bruised**: contused ▶ **flesh**: (between skin and bones) ▶ hurt, **hurt**, hurt: cause pain

wet≠dry ▶ **cloth**: piece of material (for clothes...)
lap; mother's lap on which a baby sits

assured her as he wrapped the cloth around it, 'and as soon as I'm sure you've fallen in love with me again, I'll take these off.' He straightened up and his lips grazed her ear. 'Should we call our first baby Donald, Junior?' he asked. 'I'm sure it will be a boy.'

On Thursday afternoon, Jimmy Barrott went into the office of Michael Crandell's employers, the engineering firm of Fields, Warner, Quinlan and Brown. Upon showing his badge, he was ushered into the office of Edward Fields, who was shocked to learn that Kay Crandell was missing. No, they hadn't heard from Mike today but that wasn't unusual. Mike and Kay were planning to drive back to Arizona. Mike was taking a week's vacation. Mike Crandell? Absolutely top drawer. The best. In fact, he'd just been voted into the partnership as of his completing a job that would begin next month in Baltimore. Yes, they knew Kay was upset about all the moves. Most of the wives felt that way. Would Jimmy see Mike? Tell him to let them know if there was anything they could do? Mike Crandell was the best. In every way. Did Jimmy know where Mike was staying?

Jimmy Barrott cautiously said that it was all probably a misunderstanding.

Edward Fields suddenly became very formal. 'Mr Barrott,' he said, 'if this is double-talk and you mean you're checking up on Mike Crandell, do yourself a favour and don't waste your time. I stake my own reputation and our firm's reputation on him.'

Jimmy phoned the office for messages. There were none and he went directly home. There wasn't much food in the refrigerator and he decided to go to a take-out Chinese joint. But somehow he found his car steering towards the Garden View Motel.

It was nine-thirty when he arrived there. He learned from the desk clerk that Mike had been handing out pictures of his wife to all the employees, that he had given the switchboard operator twenty dollars to give

wrapped; to wrap: to put round

these: manacles, shackles ▶ **straightened up** (to a standing position) ▶ **grazed**: touched lightly
Junior, Jnr, Jr (Am) (capital J!): used after the name of a person who has the same name as his father; John Brown Junior

upon showing (as he showed) his (detective's) **badge** he was **ushered** (shown the way) **into** the office

heard from: received news from (letters, phone calls...)
unusual: exceptional (that does not happen very often)
were planning to drive: intended to drive
a week's vacation: notice "s" in this case
top drawer: of very good quality ▶ **voted...**: admitted as a partner by a vote ▶ **as of** (as from) **completing...**: from the time he had finished... ▶ **Baltimore**, Maryland
upset: disturbed, perturbed ▶ **felt that way**: reacted in the same manner

in every way: from every point of view

cautiously; cautious: careful to avoid danger or risks
misunderstanding: error, failure to understand
become, **became**, become ▶ **formal**≠relaxed, friendly
double-talk: empty or ambiguous words
checking up on...: investigating his career, his past...
waste: lose ▶ **I stake... on him**: I risk my reputation and our firm's (reputation) on him
phoned for messages (to see if he had any message)
none: not one ▶ **directly home**: straight home
take out (take away)
Chinese **joint** (eating-house) ▶ **somehow** (not knowing why)
▶ **steering...**: directing its course in the direction of

desk clerk: receptionist ▶ **handing out**: passing out

switchboard operator (in charge of the phone in a hotel...)

his wife a message if she called. 'There was absolutely no trouble around here last night,' the clerk said nervously. 'I couldn't refuse to allow him to pass out those pictures, but this isn't the kind of publicity we want.' At Jimmy's request, the clerk produced one of the pictures, a blowup of the snapshot and underneath in large, block lettering: 'Kay Crandell is missing. She may be ill. She is 32 years old, five feet four inches, 115 pounds. Substantial reward for information about her whereabouts.' Mike's name and the phone number of the motel followed.

At ten o'clock, Jimmy knocked on the door of room 210. It was yanked open instantly and Jimmy noted the keen disappointment on Mike's face when he saw who was there. Reluctantly Jimmy conceded that Mike Crandell looked like a very worried guy. His clothes were rumpled as though he'd gotten most of his sleep in catnaps. Jimmy sauntered past him and saw the stack of photocopied pictures of Kay on the table. 'Where have you passed these out so far?' he asked.

'Mostly around the motel. Tomorrow I'm going to deliver them to train stations and bus stops in the towns around here and ask people to put them in store windows.'

'You haven't heard anything?'

Mike hesitated.

'You have heard something,' Jimmy Barrott told him. 'What is it?'

Mike pointed to the phone. 'I didn't trust the operator to remember. I put in a recorder this afternoon. Kay phoned back while I was picking up a hamburger. It must have been about eight-thirty.'

'Were you planning to let me in on that?'

'Why should I?' Mike asked. 'Why should you be bothered with... what did you call it, a domestic affair?' There was a thin edge of hysteria in his voice.

Jimmy Barrott walked over to the recorder, rewound the tape and pressed the 'play' button. The same woman's voice he had heard yesterday came on.

trouble: problem

want (here): need, look for ▶ **produced**: showed
blowup: enlargement ▶ **underneath**: under it
block lettering: separate capital letters ▶ **she may be ill**:
perhaps she is ill
pound(s): 454 grams ▶ **substantial**: large, considerable
reward: money given in return for information ▶ **whereabouts**:
place where sb is ▶ **followed**: were to be read after all the other
information
yanked open: opened suddenly and forcefully
keen: acute, intense ▶ **disappointment**: dissatisfaction
reluctantly: unwillingly ▶ **conceded**: admitted
looked like: seemed to be, resembled
rumpled: untidy, disordered, not neat ▶ **gotten** (Am): got
catnap(s), nap: short sleep; take or have a nap
stack: pile, heap
so far: up to now
mostly: for the most part, mainly, chiefly

store window (Am): shop window

you haven't heard anything?: have you got any news?

trust: count on, rely on
put in: placed ▶ **recorder**: machine for recording
phoned back: called back ▶ **picking up**: out buying
about: approximately, roughly
let me in on that (Am): tell me that (sth private)
why should I? (be planning to let you in on that?)
bothered: disturbed, given trouble
a thin edge: a little touch (hardly noticeable)
rewind,**rewound**, rewound: make go backwards
tape (made of magnetic material) ▶ **pressed the 'play' button**
(in order to listen) ▶ **voice** (which) **he had heard**

'Mike, I'm really fed up. Go home and don't leave those pictures of me around. It's humiliating. I'm here because I want to be here.' There was the sound of a receiver being slammed down.

'My wife has a soft, pretty voice.' Mike said. 'What I hear there is stress, nothing else. Forget what she's saying.'

'Look,' Jimmy said in what for him was a kindly tone. 'Women don't walk out of a marriage without some stress. I should know. Even my first wife cried at the divorce hearing and she was already pregnant by some other guy. I talked to the people you work with. They think a lot of you. Why don't you get on with your job and count your blessings? There isn't a dame worth it.'

He watched as Mike's face whitened.

'My office called.' Mike told him. 'They've offered to get a private investigator to help me. I may take them up on it.'

Jimmy Barrott leaned over and took the cassette out of the recorder. 'Can you give me the name of someone who might be able to identify your wife's voice?' he asked.

All through the night, Mike sat with his head in his hands. At six-thirty, he left the motel and drove to the train stations and bus stops in the neighbouring towns. At nine o'clock, he went to Garden State High. Classes were over for the summer but the office staff was still working. He was taken to the office of the principal, Gene Pearson. Pearson listened intently, his thin face frowning and thoughtful. 'I remember your wife well,' he said. 'I told her that if she ever wanted a job here again, it was hers. From everything her former students told me, she must have been a very good teacher.'

He'd offer Kay a job. Had she decided to take it?

'How did Kay respond to that?'

Pearson's eyes narrowed. 'As a matter of fact, she said, "Be careful, I may take you up on that." ' His

I'm... fed up (fam): I've had enough (expressing annoyance, disgust)

(telephone) **receiver ▶ slammed down**: put down abruptly
soft: quiet and pleasant to listen to
nothing else: nothing but (except) stress ▶ **forget...**: don't take any account of what she is saying
look (used to draw attention): listen ▶ **kindly**: kind-hearted
tone (of voice) ▶ **walk out of a marriage**: break a marriage

(court) **hearing** (before a judge in a lawcourt)
you work with: with whom you work
think a lot of: have a very good opinion of ▶ **get on with**: continue with ▶ **count your blessings**: be thankful for the good things you have ▶ **dame** (Am sl): woman ▶ **worth it**: worthy of respect or affection ▶ **whitened**: became white

I may take them up on it: perhaps I'll accept their offer

leaned: bent or moved his body downwards

all through...: during the whole night, throughout the night

train station(s) or railway station ▶ **neighbouring**: near the motel
over: finished, ended ▶ **staff**: personnel
taken to: 'ushered into'
intently: with careful attention
frowning: moving his eyebrows together ▶ **thoughtful**: absorbed
if she ever...: if one day...
it was hers: she could have it (the job) ▶ I conclude **from everything** her students told me...

respond to: react to
P's eyes narrowed: he almost closed his eyes; narrow≠wide
take you up on that (fam): accept your offer

attitude suddenly became formal. 'Mr Crandell, I can understand your concern, but I don't see how I can help you.' He stood up.

'Please,' Mike begged. 'There must have been pictures taken at the reunion. Did you have an official photographer?'

'Yes.'

'I want his or her name. I've got to get a full set of pictures right away. You can't refuse me that.'

His next stop was the photographer on Center Street –six blocks from the school. At least here the only issue was cost. He placed the order and went back to the motel to hear the recorder. At eleven-thirty he returned to the photographer who had made a stack of 8×10-size pictures for him from all the rolls that had been shot at the reunion–over two hundred prints in all.

The pictures under his arm, Mike drove to Virginia O'Neil's house.

All Thursday night Kay lay awake on the lumpy mattress with its harsh new sheets. Her sense that something in Donny was building up to an explosive level was all-pervasive. After she phoned and left the message for Mike, she'd cooked dinner for Donny. He had brought in cans of hash and frozen vegetables and wine. She'd gone along with him, pretending it was fun to work together.

At dinner she'd got him to talk about himself, about his mother. He'd shown her a picture of his mother, a slender blonde in her forties in a bikini that belonged on a teenager. But Kay had felt her skin prickle. There was a definite resemblance between Donny's mother and herself. They were a type, as far apart as A to Z, but a type in size and features and hair.

'She got married again, seven years ago,' Donny told her, his voice expressionless. 'Her husband works for one of the casinos in Las Vegas. He's a lot older than she is but his kids are crazy about her. They're her age.' Donny produced another picture of two men

concern: anxiety, worry
stand up, **stood up**, stood up
begged: implored, pleaded ▶ **there must have been**: there
certainly were

I've got to get (I must have) a **full** (complete) **set** (series)... (all
the pictures) ▶ **right away**: immediately

block(s) (Am): distance between two groups of buildings
issue: problem ▶ **cost**: price ▶ **placed the order**: ordered

roll(s) (of film)
shoot, shot, **shot**: take photographs ▶ **over**: more than
print(s): picture produced from a film

lumpy: full of lumps (protuberances, bumps)
harsh≠soft ▶ **sense**: (vague) feeling, impression
building up: developing, growing, increasing
level: degree ▶ **all-pervasive**: affecting her deep down;
pervade: penetrate all parts of
can(s): metal container ▶ **hash**: cooked meat cut in small pieces
frozen; **freezer** ▶ **gone along**: appeared to agree ▶ **pretending**:
acting as if ▶ **fun**: pleasure, enjoyment
she'd got him to talk: succeeded in making him talk

slender: attractively thin ▶ **in her forties**: between 40 and 49 ▶ **that
belonged...**: that a teenager would wear ▶ **prickle** (as from small
sharp points) ▶ **definite**: clearly seen
as far apart...: as different from each other as can be
features: parts of the face, external appearance

Las Vegas, Nevada; (fam) Vegas; **a lot older**: much older
are crazy about her: like her very much ▶ **they're her age**:
they're the same age as she is

in their forties with their arms around his mother. 'She's crazy about them too.'

Then he turned his attention to the food on his plate. 'You're a very good cook, Kay. I like that. My mother didn't like to cook. Most of the time I just had sandwiches. She wasn't home much.'

After dinner she played the piano and sang with him. He remembered the words to all the songs she used to teach in choir. He had opened the shutters to let in the cool night air but clearly had no fear of being heard. She asked him about that. 'Nobody comes here anymore,' he told her. 'The lake doesn't have any fish. It's too polluted for swimming. All the other houses are just rotting away. We're safe, Kay.'

When he decided it was time to go to bed, he removed the leg chain and again waited for her outside the bathroom door. When she stepped out of the shower she heard the door begin to open but when she slammed it shut, he didn't touch it again. Then as she was walking rapidly into the bedroom, Donny asked, 'What do you want for a wedding supper, Kay? We should plan something special.'

She pretended to be seriously considering the question, then shook her head and said firmly, 'I absolutely cannot make plans to get married until I have a white gown. We'll have to wait.'

'I didn't think about that, Kay,' he said as he tucked her into bed and fastened the shackle on her ankle.

She drifted in and out of sleep. Each time she woke up, it was to see Donny standing at the foot of the bed, staring at her. Her eyes would begin to open and she'd force them shut but it was impossible to deceive him. The dim light he left on in the living room shone on the pillow. 'It's all right, Kay. I know you're awake. Talk to me, darling. Are you cold? In a few days when we're married, I'll keep you warm.' At seven o'clock he brought coffee to her. She pulled herself up, careful to tuck the sheet and blanket under her arms. Her murmured 'thank you' was stilled by a kiss.

too: as well, also
turned or drew **his attention to**

she wasn't (at) **home much**
after dinner (no article!) ▶ sing, **sang**, sung; a song
the **words** (lyrics) and the tune (melody) **to** (of) the songs
(in order) **to let in** (to the room)
clearly: without doubt ▶ **had no fear**: was not afraid

fish: no plural!
swimming; swim, swam, swum; go for a swim
rotting away: falling apart (in ruins) ▶ **safe**: out of danger
removed: took away

stepped out: walked out
open: no reflexive pronoun! ▶ **slammed it shut**: shut it noisily
and with great force

wedding supper: special meal after a marriage ceremony

pretended; to pretend; pretence, false display, deception
shook her head (in protest, to express disagreement)

gown: long dress which women wear on formal occasions
tucked her into bed (comfortably, like a child)
fastened: fixed firmly
drifted...: slept on and off, not continuously ▶ **woke up**:
stopped sleeping

deceive him: make him believe she was sleeping
dim≠bright ▶ shine, **shone**, shone
pillow (on a bed for your head) ▶ **awake**≠asleep, sleeping
darling: 'honey'
keep, kept, kept
pulled herself up (straight, upright)
tuck (to make them stay in place) ▶ **blanket** (made of wool)
stilled: made quiet or calm; to still; still: quiet, calm

'I'm not going to work all day,' Donny told her.

'I was thinking all night that you said you didn't have a gown to wear to our wedding,' he told her. 'I'm going to buy you a dress today.'

The coffee cup in her hand began to tremble. With a mighty effort, Kay managed to stay calm. This might be her only chance. 'Donny, I'm sorry,' she said. 'I really don't want to seem ungrateful but the clothes you bought for me really don't fit properly. Every woman wants to select her own wedding gown.'

'I didn't think about that,' Donny said. Again he looked puzzled and thoughtful. 'That means I'd have to take you to the store. I'm not sure if I want to do that. But I'd do anything to make you happy.'

On Friday morning at six-thirty, Jimmy Barrott gave up trying to sleep and stomped into the kitchen. He made a pot of coffee, fished for a ballpoint pen on the table and started making notations on the back of an envelope.

1. Did Kay Crandell make those phone calls? Ask Virginia O'Neil to identify the voice.

2. If voice is that of Kay Crandell, check stress level with lab.

3. If Kay Crandell did make phone calls, she knew about the posters a few hours after Mike Crandell started distributing them in the motel. How?

The last question vanquished any final vestiges of sleepiness in Jimmy's brain. Could this be some kind of crazy hoax cooked up by Mike and Kay Crandell?

At ten-thirty, Jimmy Barrott was the unwilling recipient of a game of catch with two-year-old Kevin O'Neil. He tossed the ball to Kevin who caught it with one hand, but as he threw it back, Kevin yelled, 'scravits'. Jimmy missed the easy catch.

' "Scravits" is his way of putting a hex on you,' Virginia explained. She had absolutely no doubt about identifying Kay's voice. 'Except that it doesn't really sound like her,' Virginia said. 'Miss Wesley, I mean

all day: throughout the day (from beginning to end)

buy you; to buy sb sth
tremble: shake, shook, shaken
mighty: very great ▶ **managed to** + verb: succeeded in + verb + ing ▶ **stay calm**: remain calm
ungrateful≠grateful (full of gratitude)
fit: be the right size and shape ▶ **properly**: as they should
select: choose by carefully thinking which is the best

puzzled: intringued ▶ **thoughtful**: quiet and thinking a lot
take you (in my van) **to the store** (shop)
anything (possible, in my power)

six-thirty: half past six ▶ **gave up**: stopped trying to sleep
stomped: walked with heavy steps
fished for: looked for ▶ **ballpoint pen** (with a ball at the end)
making notations: writing down notes

make phone calls (not 'do'!)

check (control, verify) **stress level** (degree of stress)
lab, laboratory
did (in fact, really) **make phone calls**

how? (did she know about the posters)
vanquished: put an end to
sleepiness; sleepy: ready to fall asleep ▶ **kind**: sort
hoax: joke, trick ▶ **cooked**: concocted, made up
unwilling: not willing, reluctant ▶ **recipient**: one who receives
catch (in which a ball is thrown and caught)
tossed: threw (≠caught) ▶ catch, **caught**, caught
threw back (in his turn) ▶ **yelled**: shouted loudly ▶ **scravits**: a word invented by Kevin ▶ **missed...**: did not catch the ball although it was **easy** to do so ▶ **putting a hex on you**: using magic powers to make bad things happen to you
it doesn't sound like her: her voice is different

Mrs Crandell, oh, blazes, she kept telling me to call her Kay... Kay has such a lilt in her voice. She always sounds warm and up. That's her voice but it *isn't* her voice.'

'Where's your husband?' Jimmy asked.

Virginia looked startled. 'He's at work. He's a trader in the Mercantile Exchange.'

'You happy?'

'Of course I'm happy.' Virginia's tone was frosty. 'May I ask why that question?'

'How would you sound if you were taking off with or without your kids and dumping your husband? Stressed?'

Virginia grabbed Kevin just before he tackled his twin. 'Detective Barrott, if I were going to leave my husband, I'd sit across the table from him and tell him when and why I was leaving. And you want to know something? Kay Wesley Crandell would do it exactly the same way. It's obvious that you're projecting the way you *think* women like Kay and I act. Now if you have no further questions, I'm pretty busy.' She stood up.

'Mrs O'Neil,' he said, 'I spoke to Mike Crandell just before I came here. I understand he's ordered copies of the pictures taken at the reunion and that he'll be over here about noon with them. I'll be back at noon. In the meantime, try to remember if Kay dated anyone from around here. Or give me the names of the faculty members she was friendly with.'

Virginia separated the twins who were now fighting over custody of the available teddy bear. Her manner changed. 'I'm beginning to like you, Detective Barrott,' she told him.

The same thought that had occurred to Jimmy Barrott, that Kay knew he was showing her picture only hours after he'd passed it out at the motel, struck Mike as he drove to Virginia O'Neil's house with the stacks of pictures of the reunion.

When Virginia answered the doorbell, Mike was on

blazes: hell! (less polite) ▶ **kept telling me** (repeatedly)
...lilt...: her voice rises and falls in a pleasant way
warm: friendly, affectionate ▶ **up**: well and happy ▶ **it** *isn't* **her**
voice: there's sth srange about it, it's altered

startled: taken by surprise ▶ **a trader** buys and sells
Mercantile Exchange : *Bourse des marchandises*
(are) **you happy?**
tone (of voice) ▶ **frosty**: cold, unfriendly
why (you put) **that question?**
taking off: going away
dumping (fam): leaving, abandoning

grabbed: seized suddenly ▶ **tackled**: forced to the ground
if I were...: 'were' is the subjunctive here
across the table from him (right opposite him)

obvious: evident ▶ **projecting...**: imagining...
act: do things or behave in a particular way
no further questions: no more questions ▶ **pretty**: quite, fairly

I understand: I know, I've been told ▶ **order(ed)**: ask for sth (you
pay for)
noon: twelve o'clock, midday≠midnight
in the meantime: between now and noon ▶ **dated**: had a roman-
tic relationship with ▶ **faculty members**: teachers
be friendly with: be friends with
fighting over (about) **custody** (who would keep) the **available**
bear (the bear that was there, ready at hand)
beginning: two n's, the stress being on the second syllable
(be<u>gin</u>) ▶ **she told him**: tell sb sth
that had occurred to...: that had come into his mind

struck Mike: Mike suddenly realized that it was important
as (while) he drove; drive, **drove**, driven

doorbell (announcing visitors); to ring the doorbell

the raw edge of hysteria. The sight of Jimmy Barrott's glum face was like another turn to the already taut wire that was his nervous system.

'What are you doing here?' His blunt enquiry was almost a shout.

He was aware of Virginia O'Neil's hand on his arm; of the fact that the house seemed unnaturally quiet. 'Mike,' Virginia said, 'Detective Barrott wants to help. A couple of the other women from our class are here; we've got some sandwich makings; we'll go over the pictures together.'

For the second time in as many days, Mike felt tears welling in his eyes. This time he managed to force them back. He was introduced to the other young women, Margery, Joan and Dotty, all students of Garden State High in the years Kay had taught there. They sat together and studied the pictures Mike had brought. 'That's Bobby... he lives in Pleasantwood. That's John Durkin Kay's talking to in that picture. His wife is with him. That's...'

It was Jimmy Barrott who taped each picture to a poster-sized cardboard, marked the heads of the people in each with a number, and then had the young women identify anyone they knew. It was soon obvious that there were too many no one could remember in groups surrounding Kay.

At three o'clock, Jimmy said, 'Sorry, but we're not getting anywhere. I know you have a new principal at the school. He won't be any help to us, but is there any teacher who's been around a long time, who might be able to identify former students you people don't know?'

Virginia and her friends exchanged long, thoughtful stares. Virginia spoke for all of them. 'Marian Martin,' she said. 'She was at Garden State from the day it opened. She retired two years ago. She lives in Litchfield, Connecticut, now. She was supposed to come to the reunion but had other commitments she couldn't break.'

raw: strong but not completely developed ► **sight**: seeing

glum≠happy, cheerful ► **taut**: drawn tight≠loose ► **wire**: long thin piece of metal

blunt: not showing polite consideration ► **enquiry**: question ► **a shout**; to shout (out loud)

he was aware of...: he noticed..., he realized that...

unnaturally quiet: abnormally silent

Detective Barrott, Professor Jones, President Bush...: no articles!

sandwich makings: cheese, eggs... to make sandwiches ► **go over the pictures**: look at, examine, 'study'

for the second time in as many days (in two days) ► feel, **felt**, felt ► **tears** come out of your eyes when you are crying ► **welling**: starting to flow ► **force them back**: stop them from flowing

introduced to... (as they meet for the first time) ► **all students**: all of them (were) students

John Durkin Kay's talking to (to whom Kay is talking)

taped: stuck with (adhesive) tape

poster-sized: the size of a poster ► **cardboard** is stronger than paper ► **had** (made) **the young women identify...**

soon: in a short time

too many (students whom) **no one** (nobody) **could remember**

surround(ing): be all (a)round

we're not getting anywhere: we are not making any progress

he won't be any help (not knowing the students concerned)

who's been around...: who has been working in the school...

former students (whom) **you people** (here)

stare(s): long fixed look with the eyes wide open

retired: stopped working (given her age)

Connectitut: a state in the North East

commitment(s): sth she had arranged to do before she was asked to come ► **break**; break a promise, an agreement...

'She's the one we need,' Jimmy Barrott said. 'Does anyone have her phone number or address?'

The flicker of hope that had begun in Mike when he realized that Jimmy Barrott was on his side now leaped into a flame. People were working with him, were trying to help. *Kay, wait for me. Let me find you.*

Virginia was looking through her phone book. 'Here's Miss Martin's number.' She began dialling.

Vina Howard had accomplished a life-long ambition when she opened the 'Clothes Cartel' shop in Pleasantwood, New Jersey. She had been an assistant buyer at J C Penney's before her relentlessly unhappy marriage. When after eighteen years she'd finally left Nick Howard, she'd returned to the family home in time to nurse her two aging parents through a series of heart attacks and strokes. After they died, Vina had sold the old house, bought a small co-op, and realized her heart-hunger dream, to open a dress shop that would cater to the modern suburbanite on a budget. As an after-thought she'd added a line that would appeal to the modern suburbanite's teenage daughter. And it was that mistake that had become a daily vexation.

On Friday morning, 19 June, Vina was straightening the dresses on the rack, polishing the glass over the costume jewellery counter, giving a push and tug to the chairs near the curtained-off dressing-room area and muttering to herself. 'Horrible kids. Come in here and try on every stitch in the place. Get makeup all over the collars. Leave everything on the floor. This is the last season I cater to those slobs.'

Vina had genuine reason to be upset. She'd just had expensive new wallpaper put in the minuscule-sized changing area and some fresh kid had written the usual four-letter word all over one wall. She'd finally scrubbed it clean but the paper was blotched and shredded.

Nevertheless, the day started pleasantly enough. By ten-thirty, the time her assistant, Edna, arrived, the store was bustling and the cash register jingling.

the **one**: the person

the flicker of hope: what little brief hope he began to have
leaped into a flame: changed and grew into a flame

looking (quickly) **through ▶ phone book** (containing list of phone numbers) **▶ dialling** (the number, to make a call)

accomplish(ed) or realize an ambition **▶ life-long**: continuing through life
assistant buyer≠full buyer; buy, bought, bought
relentlessly: constantly, implacably
finally: eventually, in the end

nurse: take care of **▶ aging**: growing old
stroke(s): serious illness of the brain causing paralysis
co-op(erative apartment) (Am) (in a block, owned by each occu-pant) **▶ heart-hunger dream** (which she holds dear) **▶ cater**: provide for **▶** a **suburbanite** lives away from town centre **▶ on a budget**: who cannot afford luxuries **▶ as an afterthought**: think-ing about it later **▶ line**: type of product **▶ appeal to**: attract
mistake: error **▶ vexation**: annoyance
straightening: putting in their right or proper position
rack(s): support for holding dresses... upright (straight)
costume jewellery (made of cheap material) **▶ tug**: pull
curtained-off: separated with a curtain (hanging cloth)
muttering (against) (in a low voice) **▶** (they) **come in here**
every stitch: all the clothes **▶ makeup**: cosmetics
(they) **leave**; leave, left, left
slob(s) (fam): sb who is dirty, untidy, ill-mannered
genuine: real **▶ upset**: annoyed, vexed
expensive≠cheap **▶ wallpaper** (for covering walls)
changing area: dressing room... **▶ fresh**: impertinent, cheeky
four-letter word(s): shit, fuck, hell... **▶ scrubbed** (with brush, water) **▶ blotched**; blotch, mark **▶ shredded**: torn, cut
nevertheless: in spite of that
bustling (with people, activity) **▶ jingling** (noise) made by
cash (money) **register** (machine)

At three-fifteen there was a lull and Vina and Edna managed to have a peaceful cup of coffee. Edna promised that her husband would surely be able to stretch the leftover wallpaper to replace the damaged area in the dressing room. A visibly cheered Vina had a warm smile on her face when the door of the shop opened and a couple came in, a pretty young woman of about twenty-six or eight in a cheap-looking T-shirt and skirt and a gaunt-looking man about the same age whose arm was tightly around her. His dark-red curly hair looked as though he'd just left a hairdresser. His china-blue eyes glittered. There was something spacey about the two of them, Vina thought. Her smile tightened. There'd been a series of drug-related robberies in the area lately.

'We want a long white dress,' the man told her. 'Size eight.'

'The prom season is over,' Vina said uneasily. 'I don't have much of a selection in long dresses.'

'This one should be suitable for a wedding.'

Vina addressed herself to the young woman. 'Have you any particular style in mind?'

Desperately Kay tried to find a way to communicate with this woman. From the corner of her eye she could see that the clerk at the cash register was sensing something odd about Donny and herself. That wild-looking red wig he was wearing. She also knew that Donny's right hand was touching the gun in his pocket and that any slight effort on her part to alert these women would become their death sentence.

'Something in a cotton,' she said. 'Do you have eyelet? Or maybe a sheer jersey?' She had spotted the curtained-off dressing area. She would have to go in there alone to change... Maybe she could leave a message. The more dresses she tried on, the more time she would have.

But they had only one size eight long white eyelet dress. 'We'll take it,' Donny said.

'I want to try it on,' Kay said firmly. 'The dressing

lull: interval of calm
have a peaceful cup...: enjoy a cup, taking their time
stretch the leftover wallpaper: use what (little) wallpaper was left ▶ **damaged**; 'blotched and shredded'
cheered: comforted, made happier ▶ **warm**: welcoming, friendly

cheap-looking: which seemed to be inexpensive
gaunt: very thin and pale
tightly: firmly ▶ **dark-red**≠light red ▶ **curly**≠straight
china-blue; china, porcelain
glittered: shone brightly ▶ **spacey** (Am fam): on drugs, unconscious of what is going on ▶ **tightened**: became tense and stiff (≠relaxed) ▶ **drug-related**: connected with drug
area: district ▶ **lately**: a short time ago

the prom season (usually at the end of the academic year)
over: ended ▶ **uneasily**: feeling ill at ease
suitable: right, appropriate
have you... in mind?: are you thinking of...?

a **clerk** (Am) serves people in a store (shop) ▶ **sensing**: becoming vaguely aware of ▶ **odd**: strange ▶ **wild-looking**: most unusual, eccentric ▶ **wig**: artificial hair that he wore on his head
right≠left
slight: very small in degree, not important, insignificant
death sentence (as of the punishment of death given by a judge)

eyelet: *plumetis* ▶ **sheer**: of very thin or transparent texture
spotted: noticed
(in order) **to change** (no reflexive pronoun!)
the more..., the more...: notice the construction! ▶ **tried on** (to test the fit, to examine the appearance)
one size eight long white eyelet dress: all the words before 'dress' (except 'one') play the role of an adjective

room is right there,' she pointed out. She walked over and pulled back the curtain. 'See.'

It was barely large enough for one person. The privacy curtain did not go down to the floor. 'All right, you can try it on,' Donny said. 'I'll wait right outside.' He firmly vetoed Vina's offer to assist Kay. 'Just hand the dress in to her.'

Kay whipped off the T-shirt and skirt. Frantically she glanced around the small cubicle. A narrow shelf held a box with a couple of straight pins. But no pencil. No way to leave a message. She pulled the dress over her head, then grabbed a pin. The wallpaper on one side of the cubicle was stained and shredded. On the other side she tried to scratch the word *Help*. The pin was light. It was impossible to move it quickly. She managed a large jagged 'H'.

'Hurry up, sweetheart.'

She shoved aside the curtain. 'I can't reach these buttons in the back,' she told the salesclerk.

As she fastened the buttons, Vina glanced nervously at the cash register. Edna shook her head slightly. Get rid of them was what she was saying.

Kay studied herself in the floor-length mirror. 'I don't think it's quite right,' she said. 'Have you anything else?'

'We'll take this one,' Donny interrupted. 'You look beautiful in it.' He pulled out a wad of bills. 'Hurry up, honey,' he ordered. 'We're running late.'

Inside the cubicle, Kay stepped out of the dress, handed it around the curtain, yanked on her T-shirt and skirt and grabbed another pin. With one hand, she pretended to be fussing with her hair; with the other, she tried to begin the letter 'E' on the wallpaper but it was impossible. She whirled around when she heard Donny pull open the curtain. 'What's taking you so long, sweetheart?' he asked. Her back was to the wall where she'd begun to write. She continued to run her fingers through her hair as though trying to smooth it. She let the pin drop behind her and watched as Donny's eyes

right: directly, straight
pulled back: moved back by pulling ▶ **See**: look
barely: hardly, only just, scarcely ▶ **privacy curtain** (for iso-
lation)

vetoed: refused, rejected ▶ **assist**: help ▶ **hand**: pass

whipped off: suddenly took off ▶ **frantic(ally)**, frenetic
glanced: looked briefly ▶ **cubicle**: small enclosed compartment
held: contained ▶ **straight**≠curved ▶ **pin(s)**: short pointed piece
of metal for fastening together pieces of cloth
grabbed; to gra<u>b</u>: to seize suddenly
stained and shredded: 'blotched and shredded'
to scratch: make marks, lines with sth pointed
light≠heavy ▶ **move it**: make it change position
managed (to write) a **jagged** (irregular) 'H'

shoved aside (fam): pushed to one side ▶ **reach**: get hold of
salesclerk (Am): sales assistant (who sells things)
fasten(ed)≠unfasten, undo
shook her head (disapprovingly) ▶ **slightly**: a little
get rid of them: make them leave (they'll cause problems**)**
floor-length: reaching to the floor
it's quite right (in size, colour...)

a wad of bills: a thick pile of banknotes
we're running late: we are getting late (in our timetable)
stepped out of the dress; step, move one foot after the other
yanked on: put on suddenly and quickly

fussing with...: doing her hair and 'making a big thing of it' (see
bottom of page 16)
whirled around: turned round fast
pull open: open by pulling ▶ **so long**: such a long time
to the wall: facing the wall
to run (move) **her fingers through her hair**
smooth it: make it smooth (≠rough, uneven) ▶ **she let the pin
drop** (fall) or she dropped the pin

took in the tiny cubicle. Then, apparently satisfied, he took her hand and with the box under his arm hurried her from the store.

Marian Martin had just completed planting her new azaleas when the pealing of the phone summoned her into the house. She was a tall, sixty-seven-year-old woman with a trim, disciplined body, close-cropped hair that curled around her face, lively brown eyes and a kind, no-nonsense manner. In the two years since she had retired from her position as head guidance counsellor at Garden State High and moved to this quiet Connecticut town, she'd joyfully indulged herself in the avocation she'd never had enough time for. Now her English garden was her unabashed pride. The telephone call that Friday afternoon was not therefore a welcome interruption, but after she finished listening to Virginia O'Neil, Marian forgot about her unplanted dahlias.

Kay Wesley, she thought. A born teacher. She'd always been willing to take on kids who weren't doing well. All her students were crazy about her. Kay, *missing*. 'I have a couple of errands,' she told Virginia. 'But I can be on my way by six. It should take about two hours. Have the pictures ready. There isn't a kid who went to Garden State whose face I don't know.'

As she hung up, Marian was struck by the memory of Wendy Fitzgerald, the Garden State senior who twenty years ago had vanished during a school picnic. Her murderer had been Rudy Kluger, the school handyman. Rudy must be due out of prison around now. Marian's mouth went dry. Not that, please.

At five-forty-five, her overnight bag tossed in the back of her car, she was on her way to New Jersey. Details of that horrible time from the moment Wendy Fitzgerald was reported missing to the day her body was found filled Marian's mind. So engrossed was she in her apprehension about Rudy that she pushed deep

took in: observed ▶ **tiny**: minuscule, miniscule
hurried her...: made her leave the store quickly

completed planting: finished planting
the pealing...: the telephone ringing ▶ **summoned her into the house**: made her go...
trim: thin, with no extra fat ▶ **close-cropped**: cut very short
curled: was curly (≠straight) ▶ **lively**: full of life
no-nonsense: efficient, concentrating on important matters
head guidance...: counsellor at the head of the other counsellors
moved: moved house ▶ **quiet**: peaceful
indulged herself in the avocation: allowed herself to enjoy the pastime (hobby) (**for** which she had never had time)
unabashed pride (she gloried in her garden and she was not ashamed of doing so) ▶ **therefore**: in consequence
welcome: received with pleasure
unplanted: which she had not planted

a born teacher: one who has a strong natural ability to teach
take on: accept in her class ▶ **doing well**: successful academically
crazy about: very fond of her
errand(s): short journey to buy things...
be on my way: leave here ▶ **by six**: not later than six
have the pictures ready: get the pictures ready

hung up: put the receiver down ▶ **struck...**: suddenly remembered ▶ **senior** (Am): student in his last year
vanished: disappeared
handyman: man who does repairs and practical jobs
be due (at a particular time..., as expected, as arranged)
dry (with anxiety) ▶ (may) **not that** (happen to Kay)
overnight bag (that you take when you go and stay somewhere)
tossed: thrown in a quick, careless way

engrossed: absorbed ('details... filled her mind')
pushed deep (deeply)

into her subconscious the fleeting thought that some
incident involving Kay was eluding her.

Virginia put the receiver down. 'Miss Martin should
be here around eight,' she said.

Jimmy Barrott pushed back his chair. 'I've gotta
check in at the office. If this guidance counsellor
comes up with anything tonight, anything at all, call
this number. Otherwise, I'll be back in the morning.'
He handed Virginia a somewhat dog-eared card.

The other young women stood up as well. They too
would come back to work with Miss Martin tomorrow.

Mike stood up. 'I'll get more flyers around. Then
I'll go back to the motel. There's always the chance
Kay will phone again.'

This time he tacked Kay's pictures on telephone
poles in the main streets of the towns he drove through
and in the large shopping malls in the area. In Pleasantwood he had a near brush with a van that hurtled past
him as he drove into the municipal parking lot. Damn
fool, Mike thought. He'll kill someone.

Donny had parked the van in the municipal lot behind
the Clothes Cartel. When they left the store, he kept
his arm tightly around Kay until they reached the van,
then he opened the side door and nudged her forward.
Frantically, Kay looked at the burly young man about
to start his car two parking spaces away. For an instant
she made eye contact with him, then felt the tip of the
gun pressed against her side. 'There's a little kid in the
back of that car, Kay,' Donny said softly. 'You make
a sound and that guy and the kid are dead.'

Her legs turned to rubber as she stumbled up the
step. 'Here's the package, honey,' Donny said loudly.
He watched as the nearby car passed them, then jumped into the van and yanked the door shut.

'You wanted to signal that guy, Kay,' he hissed. The
gag that he shoved in her mouth was cruelly tight. His
hands were rough as he snapped on the handcuffs,

fleeting: brief, passing (≠lasting)
involving Kay: including Kay ▶ **was eluding her**: escaped her

put the receiver down: 'hung up', rang off
around eight: at about eight (approximately)
pushed back his chair (in its former position) ▶ **I've gotta** (Am): I have got to ▶ **check in** (and see what's going on)
comes up with: thinks of ▶ **anything at all** (however unimportant, apparently) ▶ **otherwise**: if she does not
somewhat: to some degree ▶ **dog-eared**: with the corners turned over ▶ **as well**: in their turn

get... around: deliver, hand out, distribute ▶ **flyer(s)**: poster
chance: possibility of sth happening (of Kay phoning again)

tacked: fixed in place with a tack (with a sharp point)
main street(s)≠side street ▶ **through** which he drove
shopping mall(s) (Am): shopping centre (often enclosed)
he had a near brush: he nearly hit ▶ **hurtled past him**: passed him very quickly in a rough violent way ▶ **damn fool**: stupid ass
kill someone: make sb die

store (Am): shop; store, large department store in Britain (like Selfridge's, Harrods...) ▶ **reached**: arrived at, got to
nudged: moved by gently pushing ▶ **forward(s)**≠backward(s)
burly: big and strong ▶ (who was) **about to start**
parking space(s): 'spot'
made eye contact with...: their eyes met ▶ **tip**: extremity
kid (fam): child
back≠front ▶ **softly**: in a low gentle voice (no less menacingly)
make a sound: shout or say anything
turned to (changed into) ▶ **rubber** (of which car tyres are made)
stumbled (nearly falling) **up the step** (into the van) ▶ **package** (containing the dress) ▶ **nearby**: near in position
yanked the door shut: slammed the door shut (violently)
signal: communicate with a signal ▶ **hissed** (in a quiet angry voice) ▶ **shoved**: pushed brutally ▶ **tight**≠loose
rough: not gentle, violent ▶ **snapped on**: roughly put on

shackled her feet and looped the chain through them. He dropped the box beside her on the cot. 'Just remember why we bought that dress, Kay, and don't make eyes at other men.' He opened the door a crack, looked around, then pushed the door a little wider and slipped out. In the moment that light filtered into the van, Kay's glance fell on a long, thin object on the floor beneath the worktable.

A screwdriver.

If she had the screwdriver, she might be able to unfasten the metal plate from the wall in the cottage, might have a chance to get away while Donny was at work.

The van leaped forward. Donny had to be at the breaking point to drive this fast. Let the police see him, she prayed, please. But then the van slowed perceptibly. He must have realized he was driving too fast.

She turned on her side, slowly dropped her manacled hands and with her fingertips tried to reach the screwdriver. Angry, frustrated tears blurred her eyes and impatiently she shook them away. In the near dark, she could barely make out the thin, long outline of the tool, but no matter how desperately she tried, until the handcuffs burned her wrist bones, it was beyond her reach.

She rolled onto her back and dragged her hands up until they rested on her knees. The cot creaked as she worked her way to a sitting position, swung her legs down, wiggled her body until she was at the very edge of the cot and stretched her legs towards the screwdriver. It was less than an inch beyond her reach. Ignoring the searing pain as the shackles bit into her legs, she pointed the toes of her sandals until she felt the thin blade, then grasped it between the soles of her sandals and pulled the screwdriver back towards the cot. Finally it was directly below her. She swung her legs up, fell onto her back and again dropped her hands over the side towards the floor. The bruised flesh sent angry pain signals that she no longer felt because her fingers were closing around the handle of the screwdriver, closing around it, holding it, lifting it up.

looped: fastened with a loop (a curve crossing itself)
dropped: lay down ▶ **beside**: next to ▶ **cot** (Am): camp bed
(usually collapsible) ▶ **make eyes at**: look amorously at
... a crack (very slightly)≠**a little wider**
slipped out (quietly)
filtered (only slightly, a little) **into the van**
glance: brief look
beneath: under ▶ **worktable** (at which a workman works)
a **screwdriver** is a long thin tool for turning screws

unfasten: detach ▶ **cottage**: the 'frame house' p 30
get away: leave, flee
leaped (moved quickly) **forward** ▶ **at the breaking point**:
(nervously and be unable to go on) ▶ as **fast** as this ▶ **let** or may
the police see him, she prayed (to God) ▶ **slowed**: ran more
slowly
manacled: with the manacles or handcuffs on
her fingertips: the extremities of her fingers ▶ **reach**: get at
blurred: caused her eyes to see less distinctly
shook them away: removed them by shaking (trembling)
make out: see clearly ▶ **outline**: shape, form
no matter how...: in spite of her desperate efforts...
burned (like fire) ▶ **wrist**: joint between hand and arm ▶ **it was
beyond her reach**: she could not reach it ▶ **dragged her hands
up** (with difficulty) ▶ **rested**: lay
worked her way...: sat after great effort ▶ **swung her legs down**
(in a curve) ▶ **wiggled...** (by twisting and turning it) ▶ **at the very
edge**: right at the edge ▶ **stretched**: extended
1 inch: 2.54 cm ▶ **beyond**: farther than ▶ **reach**: act of reaching
searing: burning ▶ **bit into** (as if with teeth)
toe(s) (here): forepart (front part) ▶ **thin**≠thick
blade (here): metal part ▶ **grasped**: seized ▶ **sole(s)**: under sur-
face ▶ **towards**: in the direction of
directly: right, straight ▶ **below**: under ▶ swing, **swung**,
swung ▶ **fell onto her back**: lay down on her back

angry (inflamed) **pain**
closing around: gradually surrounding ▶ **handle** (for holding it)
lifting it up (in a higher position), raising it

For a moment she rested, gasping from the effort, exulting in her victory. Then her fingers tightened on the tool as a new thought struck her. How could she get it into the house? There was no place to hide it on her person. The cheap T-shirt clung to her body; the cotton skirt had no pockets; the sandals were open.

They were nearly at the cabin. She could feel the movement of the van as it twisted and turned and bumped along the dirt road. The dress box flipped over and brushed her arm. *The dress box.* The clerk had tied the string around the box with a double knot. She couldn't possibly undo it. Carefully, Kay slipped her fingers between the lid and the bottom of the box, then slowly began to work the screwdriver into the opening her fingers had made. She felt the lid tear at the side.

The van stopped. Desperately she pushed the screwdriver in, trying to force it between the folds of the dress, and managed to flip the box on its side before the door opened. 'We're home, Kay,' Donny said tonelessly.

She prayed that he wouldn't notice the angry new marks on her wrists and ankles, the tear in the box. But his movements when he unlocked the chain and cuffs were automatic. He slung the box under his arm without glancing at it, unlocked the cabin door and pushed her inside quickly as though he was afraid of being followed. The inside of the cabin was stifling.

Every instinct told Kay that somehow she must try to calm him. 'You're hungry,' she told him. 'You haven't eaten for hours.' She'd fixed lunch when he returned to the cabin at one o'clock but he was too agitated to eat. 'I'll make a sandwich for you and some lemonade,' she said. 'You need it.'

He dropped the dress box on the couch and stared at her. 'Tell me how much you love me,' he ordered. His eyes were wide-pupilled now; his grip on her wrists tighter than the handcuffs had been. His breath came in short, uneven gasps. Terrified, Kay stepped back until the rough velour of the couch touched her

rested: ceased (from tiring activity) ▶ **gasping**: breathing with difficulty; to breathe: to take in air (into your lungs)

struck her: suddenly occurred to her (crossed her mind)

hide, hid, hidden: prevent from being seen

cling, **clung**, clung: adhered closely to her body

open: not covered

cabin: 'frame-house', 'cottage'

twisted, turned (zigzagged), **bumped** (along a bad road)

dirt road (without any gravel or tarmac) ▶ **flipped over**: suddenly turned over ▶ **brushed**: touched

tied: fastened ▶ **string**: fine cord ▶ **knot**: string... twisted together and tied ▶ **undo**≠tie, fasten ▶ **slipped**: pushed with a quick movement ▶ **lid**: cover ▶ **bottom**≠top

work into: introduce by gradual movement ▶ **opening**: passage

tear: get pulled apart; tear, tore, torn

fold(s): *pli*

flip the box (a transitive verb here): turn it over

tonelessly; a toneless voice does not express any feelings

notice: see; take notice of: pay attention to

the **tear** in the box: 'tear' is a noun here!

unlocked: undid, unfastened ▶ **cuffs**: handcuffs

sling, **slung**, slung: throw carelessly or with force

unlocked: undid the lock of the door (using a key)

as though: as if (more often used in spoken English)

stifling: vey hot and difficult to breathe in

somehow: in one way (still unknown) or another

you're hungry; be hungry; be thirsty

fixed (fam): to fix a meal, to prepare a meal

make a sandwich: not 'do'! also 'make' a drink

lemonade (Am): made from lemons (*citrons*), sugar, and water

he ordered (using his authority or power)

wide-pupilled: with wide pupils ▶ **grip**: firm hold

(was) **tighter** ▶ **breath** (noun); to breath<u>e</u>

uneven: irregular; **gasp(s)** is a noun here

rough, stiff≠smooth ▶ **touched**: brushed

legs. He was about to come apart. He would know immediately if she tried to placate him with lies. Instead she said crisply, 'Donny, I'd like to hear more about why *you* love *me*. You say you do, but you always get angry at me. How can I believe you anymore? Read to me from one of your books while I get us something to eat.' She forced a note of cold authority into her voice. 'Donny, I want you to read to me *now*.'

'Of course, I'll read, Miss Wesley.' His voice lost the hard edge of anger, became higher-pitched, almost adolescent. 'But first I have to check my messages.'

He had left the phone on the table by the couch when they went out. Now he took a notebook and pencil from his pocket and pressed the 'play' button. There were three messages. One from a hardware store; could Donny come in tomorrow? Their repairman was out sick. One from the Garden View Motel. They needed extra help installing some electronic equipment for a seminar. They really needed him to work through the evening.

The last call was obviously from an elderly man. There was a distinct wheeze in his halting voice as he identified himself. Clarence Gerber. Could Donny stop by and take a look at the toaster? It wouldn't heat up and the wife was burning all the bread trying to make toast in the oven. A laboured laugh followed and a 'Put us on the top of the list, Donny. Call and let me know when you're coming.'

Donny put his notebook away, rewound the tape and this time stood on the couch to set the recorder in the wire box. 'I can't stand that old guy, Gerber,' he told Kay. 'No matter how many times I tell him not to –when I'm fixing something of his–he gets in the van and keeps talking to me while I work. And I have to go to the motel first. They pay me on the spot. I've saved a lot of money for us, Kay.' He got down from the couch. 'And now I'll read to you. Show me which books you haven't seen yet.'

'I sensed from that first day in choir, when Kay put

come apart: fall into a bad mental state
placate: make him stop feeling angry ▶ **lie(s)**: untruth ▶ **instead** (of trying to placate him) ▶ **crisply**: brusquely

believe; believe in God
get us something to eat: 'fix' sth to eat

now : right now, immediately (hence the italics)
Miss Wesley (as if he was her student again)
hard edge≠gentle tone ▶ **higher-pitched**≠deeper
check my messages: see, make sure if I have any message

'play' button; play a cassette, a CD, a record
hardware: household equipment and tools, nails, locks...
out sick: out of work, being sick (ill)

extra help: more help ▶ **installing**: in order to install
through the evening: all evening, throughout the evening

obviously: clearly ▶ **elderly**: old or becoming old
wheeze: sound as of sb with asthma ▶ **halting**: slow and hesitating ▶ **identified himself**: gave his name ▶ **stop by** (for a short time) ▶ **toaster** (for bread) ▶ **it wouldn't heat up**: it did not get or become hot (nothing doing!)
oven; microwave oven ▶ **laboured** (given the 'wheeze')
on the top of the list (to be served first)

put away... (after using it) ▶ **rewound...** (backwards)
to set,set, set: to put, to place
wire box: 'the padlocked wire cage' (p 48) ▶ **stand**: bear
no matter...: however often... ▶ **not to** (get in the van...)
fixing: mending ▶ **something of his**: one of his things
keeps talking (on and on, endlessly)
first: before anything else ▶ **on the spot**: immediately
saved: amassed; save money in a bank

I sensed...: I vaguely felt that...

her hands on my chest and told me to sing, that there was something special and beautiful between us,' Donny read as he sipped the lemonade. His voice calmed as he spoke of the many times she had phoned him and asked him to come to her. As she sat opposite him, Kay found it almost impossible to swallow. Over and over he repeated how happy he would be to die with her, how glorious it would be to die defending his right to her.

He finished reading and smiled. 'Oh, I forgot,' he said. Reaching up, he pulled off the curly red wig, revealing his balding head of skimpy brown hair. He leaned down and for the first time removed the blue contact lenses. His own eyes, muddy brown with odd flecks of green, stared at her. 'Do you love me best when I'm the real me?' he asked. Without waiting for an answer he came around the table and pulled the chair. 'I've got to go to the motel. I'll get you settled in the living room, Kay.'

At the Clothes Cartel, Vina Howard and her assistant Edna spent a gossipy five minutes discussing the couple who had bought the white eyelet dress. 'I swear the two of them were on drugs,' Edna volunteered. 'But listen, we both agreed that dress was a mistake. You were about to reduce it, right? So now you got full price. And cash at that.'

Vina agreed. 'But I still say he was weird-looking. He dyes his hair. I could swear it.' The door opened and a new customer came in. Vina helped her select several skirts, then led her to the dressing area. Her burst of indignation startled both Edna and the customer. 'Look,' Vina exploded. With a trembling finger she pointed to the jagged *H* on the wall. 'She was worse than he was,' she fumed. 'Now we won't have enough paper to fix both walls. I wish I had my hands on her.' Even the customer's sympathetic exclamations and Edna again pointing out that she had sold the eyelet dress full price did not placate Vina's sense of outrage.

chest: upper front part of the human body

sipped; to sip: to drink slowly, taking very small mouthfuls
as (while) **he spoke ► phoned him**: no preposition!
opposite him: in front of him, facing him
impossible to swallow *(avaler)* (feeling so nervous) **► over and over** (again): many times, repeatedly

right: something one may have or do
forget, **forgot**, forgotten
reaching up: moving up his hand **► pulled off**: removed
balding: getting bald (hairless) **► skimpy**: small in quantity
leaned (Am), leant: bent down
muddy, dull≠bright **► odd**: strange, unusual
fleck(s): small mark or spot **► love me best**: prefer me
the real me (without a wig, without contact lenses)

I've (got) to go: I must go **► settl(ed)**: put carefully in a particular place

(shop) **assistant**
gossipy: informal and full of gossip (small talk about other people's private affairs) **► I swear**: I'm certain, I bet
volunteer(ed): tell sb sth without being asked
both: the two of us **► make a mistake** (not 'do'!)
reduce it: sell it at a reduced (≠full) price **► right?**: weren't you?
cash: ready money **► at that**: too, what's more
I still say: I maintain **► weird**: strange, odd, pecular
dyes his hair: gives it a different colour; to dye(≠to die)
customer (buying things) **► helped her (to) select** (choose)
led her to...: took her to; lead, led, led
burst: sudden loud sound **► startled...**: made them start (make a sudden movement) **► exploded**, burst with anger
jagged (roughly written by Kay)
worse≠better **► she fumed**: she said angrily
I had (subjunctive) my hands...: I could get hold of her
sympathetic: compassionate, full of understanding
pointing out that: drawing her attention to the fact that
placate: appease **► sense of outrage**: feeling of indignation

Vina continued to churn inwardly to the point that at six o'clock when she closed the shop and started to walk the three blocks home, she stared straight at the poster dangling from the telephone pole and it did not register on her consciousness that the woman whose face she was seeing was the same miserable creature who had wrecked the rest of her wallpaper.

It was nearly nine o'clock when Mike arrived back at the Garden View Motel. The night had become hot and muggy and beads of perspiration formed on his forehead as soon as he left the air-conditioned car. He began walking towards the motel. A wave of dizziness made him stop and steady himself against the car he was passing, a dark-grey van. He realized that he'd eaten nothing since the sandwich at Virginia's home. He went directly to the room and checked the recorder. There were no messages.

The coffee shop was still open. Only three or four booths were occupied. He ordered a sliced-steak sandwich and coffee. The waitress offered a sympathetic smile. 'You're the one whose wife is missing. Good luck. I'm sure it will turn out fine. I have a feeling.'

'Thank you.' *I wish to God I had that feeling*, Mike thought. On the other hand, at least people were noticing Kay's picture.

The waitress left him and returned with a take-out bag and a check for the man seated two booths away. 'Working late tonight, aren't you, Donny?' she asked.

It was after six o'clock when Donny pulled away in the van. As soon as the sound of the engine faded Kay worked her hand into the dress box for the screwdriver. If she could free the metal plate from the wall, she might be able to get to the phone. But as she studied the thick padlock on the cage, she knew that would be hopeless. It was the metal plate or nothing.

She pulled herself over to the plate and crouched on the floor. The screws were so tightly in place they

churn inwardly (inside): be violently disturbed, angry
closed the shop (at closing time); to close, to shut

dangling: hanging loosely ▶ **it did not register on her consciousness that...**: she did not realize or notice that...
miserable (used to describe sb you do not like)
wrecked: damaged, ruined

become, became, **become**
muggy: unpleasantly warm and wet ▶ **bead(s)**: small drop
forehead: part of face above eyes ▶ **as soon as**: right after
dizziness; feel dizzy, lose one's balance and be about to fall
steady himself: get back his balance in order to prevent himself from falling

checked the recorder (to find out if there was any message)

coffee shop: restaurant selling drinks and light meals
booth(s): partly enclosed place ▶ **sliced**; a slice: a thin, flat piece
waitress: female waiter ▶ **offered...**: gave him...
(I wish you) **good luck** (good fortune)
turn out fine: end well ▶ **I have a feeling**, the impression (that it will turn out fine) ▶ **I wish to God**: I strongly wish
on the other hand (even if he didn't have that feeling) ▶ **at least** (if nothing else happens)
a take-out bag (containing food you take out or take away)
check (Am) (showing how much you must pay) ▶ **seated**: sitting
(You're) **working late tonight, aren't you?**

pulled away: started moving forward (in his van)
engine: motor ▶ **faded**: gradually disappeared from hearing
worked her hand (with efforts) into the dress box **for** (trying to get) the screwdriver ▶ **free**: detach, unfasten, loosen
get to: reach (and get hold of) ▶ **studied**: examined
on the cage (containing the recorder-phone) (p 48)
hopeless: without hope (absolutely impossible)
crouched (with arms and legs close to the body)

might have been welded to the plate. The screwdriver was small. Minutes passed, a half hour, an hour. Unaware of the heat, of the perspiration that soaked her body, of the exhaustion in her fingers, she worked on. Finally she was rewarded. One of the screws began to turn. With paralyzing slowness, it yielded. Finally, it was completely loose. Carefully she tightened it just enough to keep it from wobbling and began on the next screw. How much time had passed? How long would Donny be gone?

After a while numbness took over. She worked like a robot, unheeding of the pain shooting through her hands and arms, the cramps in her legs. She had just felt the second screw begin to move when she realized that the faint sound she had heard was the van. Frantically she dragged herself to the couch, slipped the screwdriver into the springs and picked up the book Donny had left on the couch.

The door creaked open. Donny's heavy footsteps resounded across the floorboards. He was holding a bag in his hand. 'I brought you a hamburger and a soda, Kay,' he told her. 'I saw Mike Crandell in the coffee shop. Your picture is all over the place. It wasn't a good idea for you to make me take you shopping. We're going to move up our wedding a day. I have to go to the motel in the morning–they'll think it's funny if I don't show up. And they owe me money. But when I come back, we'll get married and clear out of here.'

The decision seemed to have made him calm. He walked over to her and put the bag on the couch. 'Aren't you glad that whenever I get something for myself, I think of you?' His kiss on her forehead was lingering.

Kay tried not to show revulsion. At least in the dim light he wouldn't notice how swollen her hands were. And he was going to the motel to work tomorrow morning. That meant she had just a few hours left before she disappeared with him.

Donny cleared his throat. 'I'm going to be such a

(that) **they might...** ▶ **welded**: pressed together when hot
unaware of: unconscious of
heat; hot ▶ **soak(ed)**: make completely wet
exhaustion: extreme tiredness ▶ **worked on**: kept working
she was rewarded (her efforts paid)
slowness; slow≠fast ▶ **yielded**: gave way
loose: free ▶ **tightened it**: fastened it by turning
keep from: stop from ▶ **wobbling**: moving from side to side (and
falling); to wobble
be gone: be absent
numbness: inability to feel (pain) ▶ **took over**: suceeded
unheeding of≠reacting to ▶ (very sharp) pain **shooting**
(moving suddenly and quickly through)

faint: hardly audible
dragged herself to... (with difficulty) ▶ **slipped**: put quickly
(the wire) **spring(s)**: twisted pieces of metal

creaked open: opened with a creaking sound ▶ **heavy**≠light
footstep(s) (taken when walking) ▶ **floorboard(s)** (made of
wood) ▶ bring, **brought**, brought
soda or soda pop (Am)
all over the place: everywhere

move up... a day: arrange for our wedding to take place one day
earlier ▶ **funny**: strange
show up (fam): arrive, come, turn up (fam) ▶ **they owe me
money**: they have to pay me (for my work) ▶ **clear out of here**
(fam): leave here ▶ **made him calm**: calmed him down

whenever is emphatic for 'when': every single time

lingering (not 'prim' this time): long, slow to end
dim: faint≠bright
swollen: grown bigger than usual; swell, swelled, swollen

meant (to say); mean, meant, meant
disappeared: 'cleared out'
cleared his throat (*gorge*) (to be able to speak clearly)

nervous bridegroom, Kay,' he said. 'Let's practise our wedding vows now. "I, Donald, take thee, Kay..." '

He had totally memorized the traditional marriage service. Kay's mind was filled with the memory of saying, 'I, Katherine, take thee, Michael.' Oh Mike, she thought, Mike.

'Well, Kay?' The edgy tone was returning to Donny's voice.

'I don't have as good a memory as you,' she said. 'Maybe you'd better write the words down so I can practise tomorrow when you're at work.'

Donny smiled. In the dim, shadowy light, his eyes seemed deep in their sockets, his face thin to the point of being skeletal. 'I think that would be nice,' he said. 'Now, why don't you eat your hamburger?'

That night Kay kept her eyes resolutely closed, forced her breathing to sound even. She was aware of Donny drifting back and forth and watching her, but her mind was focused only on the fact that even if she did manage to get the metal plate loose before he came back, there was no guarantee that she could escape him. How far could she go in these unfamiliar woods, with one foot shackled and carrying the weight of the plate and the chain?

The traffic was heavy on Route 95 South. At six-thirty, Marian Martin realized that the slight, persistent headache she was developing was probably the result of having eaten only a small sandwich for lunch. A cup of tea and a roll, she thought longingly. But the sense of urgency that was steadily building within her kept her foot on the accelerator until at seven-fifty she pulled into the driveway of Virginia O'Neil's home in Jefferson Township.

Virginia had cheese and crackers and a chilled decanter of wine waiting in the living room. Gratefully Marian nibbled the brie, sipped Chablis and absorbed the pleasantly furnished room with its grand piano covered with sheet music in one alcove.

bridegroom: man on his wedding day
vow(s): solemn promise ► **thee** is archaic for 'you'
memorized: learnt by heart
mind: brain (that people use to think) ► **filled <u>with</u>**: full <u>of</u>

edgy: nervous and worried, tense

as good **a** memory as you: notice the position of the article!
so (Am): so that
when you<u>'re</u> at work: no future after 'when, while'...
shadowy: full of shadows (intercepting rays of light)
socket(s): cavity holding eye
skeletal: like a skeleton ► **nice** (here): a good thing to do
now indicates that he wants her attention: look

even: regular, steady; **she was aware of...**: she realized that
Donny was **dritfting back and forth** (walking up and down more
or less uncontrollably) ► **focused**: concentrated
did manage: really managed ► **get... loose**: free, unfasten

unfamiliar: unknown to her ► **woods** (round the 'clearing')
weigh<u>t</u>; to weigh (no t!): to measure how heavy sth is

the traffic was heavy: there were lots of vehicles on...
a slight headache≠a bad headche; backache, toothache...
developing; develop an illness: become affected by it

roll: small round loaf of bread ► **longing(ly)**: strong desire
stead<u>i</u>ly; steady, constant ► **building**: becoming greater, increasing ► **pulled into** (of a vehicle): moved into
driveway: private road (between a house and the street)

chilled: made cool or cold
decanter: glass container ► **gratefully**: with gratitude
nibbled, sipped (in small quantity) ► **absorbed**: took in
furnished with table... ► **grand piano**≠upright piano
sheet music (printed on paper) ► **alcove**: recess (niche)

The sheet music triggered Marian's memory. 'You played the piano in Kay Wesley's choir class, didn't you?'

'Not for the whole year. Just the last semester Kay taught.'

'*What am I trying to remember about that class?*' Marian wondered aloud, impatiently.

Dinner was a lemon-chicken casserole with a wild-rice mix and a salad, but hungry as she was, Marian barely knew what she was swallowing. She insisted on studying the reunion pictures while she ate. Rudy Kluger had been tall and thin. He'd been in his early thirties when he murdered Wendy Fitzgerald. That means he'd be in his fifties now. Marian skimmed the pictures quickly. The earliest graduates would be about forty. There shouldn't be too many older men in the photos.

There weren't. The few she saw did not remotely resemble Rudy. As she went through the pictures, Virginia filled her in on the fact that Mike was distributing Kay's picture in local towns, that the detective on the case at first seemed to doubt this was a legitimate disappearance but now was actively helpful. 'He'll be at his office till pretty late tonight, I gather,' Virginia said. 'He told me to phone if we think we've come across anything.' She moved her chair to sit next to Marian as Jack cleared the table and set out coffee cups. Virginia picked up one picture. 'You see,' she said, 'this was right at the end. Kay had just finished a hot dog. She started saying goodbye to the people around her. I was the last one she spoke to. Then she walked through the path to the parking lot.'

Marian studied the picture. Kay was standing very near the path. But something caught Marian's eye in the woods leading to the parking lot. 'Have you a magnifying glass?' she asked.

A few minutes later, they were in agreement. Almost hidden behind a big elm tree near the parking lot, was something that might be a man trying to avoid being seen. 'This probably means absolutely nothing,'

triggered...: caused her memory to work; to trigger, to set in action

whole: entire, complete ▶ **semester** (Am): one of the two divisions of the academic year

wondered: asked herself ▶ **aloud** (as if speaking to herself)
lemon (yellow fruit with acid juice)**-chicken casserole** (the bird being cooked slowly in a casserole, a covered dish) ▶ **wildrice**: *riz sauvage* ▶ **swallowing** (down into her stomach)

in his early thirties: between 31 and 35 years old
murdered: killed; a murderer
skimmed: went through rapidly, examined quickly
graduate (Am): student who has successfully completed high school and has received a certificate or diploma
there weren't (any older men) ▶ **not remotely**: not at all

filled her in on the fact: informed her of the fact
local: 'surrounding' ▶ **on the case**: in charge of the investigation
▶ **a legitimate disappearance**, a case that can be defended, not just a 'domestic affair' (p 36)
pretty: quite, rather, fairly ▶ **I gather**: I suppose, I think, I guess (Am)
come across: discovered, found out
cleared the table (dinner being over) ▶ **set out**: put (on the table) ▶ **picked up**: took
right at (immediately before) **the end**: at the very end

the last one she spoke to: the last one to whom she spoke
path (for pedestrians, through woods, across fields...)
standing; stand, stood, stood
caught Marian's eye (attracting her attention)
leading to: that led to; lead, led, led
magnifying glass (used to make objects look bigger)
they... in agreement: they agreed (shared the same opinion)
hidden: made invisible ▶ **elm tree**: *orme*
avoid being...: take action in order to prevent being seen

Marian said, trying to keep her voice steady. 'But maybe it would be a good idea for me to talk to that detective now.'

Jimmy Barrott was at his desk when the call came. He was as a matter of fact studying the file of one Rudy Kluger who twenty years ago had 'killed and murdered' a sixteen-year-old student of Garden State High after waylaying her in the woods near the picnic area. Rudy Kluger had been released from Trenton State Prison six weeks ago and had already violated his parole by not reporting to his parole officer.

Jimmy Barrott felt a weight settle in his chest as he listened to the former guidance counsellor tell him that in one picture she thought she saw someone lurking in the woods just as Kay Crandell was leaving and that she had this horrible worry about Rudy Kluger.

'Miss Martin,' Jimmy Barrott said, 'I'll tell you straight. Rudy Kluger is out of jail. We've got an alert out for him now. But will you do me a favour? Pretend that Kluger doesn't exist. Go over those pictures with an open mind. I don't know why, but I have a feeling you're going to come up with something that will help us.'

He was absolutely right about having an open mind, she knew. Marian hung up the phone and began studying the pictures again.

At eleven-thirty, she could not keep her eyes open. 'I'm not as young as I used to be,' she said apologetically.

The guest room was at the other end of the second floor from the nursery. Even so, Marian vaguely heard one of the twins wailing in the middle of the night. She fell back to sleep but in that brief wakening time realized that something was bothering her, something she had seen in the photos that was absolutely vital to remember.

Clarence Gerber did not sleep well that Friday night. There was nothing Brenda enjoyed more for breakfast

keep her voice steady ('even'), speak in a very controlled way

desk: writing table ► **the call came**: the telephone rang
file: collection of information ► **one...**: a certain Rudy...

murdered: deliberately and illegally killed
waylay(ing): wait for and stop sb, especially to rob them or attack
them ► **released**: let free, allowed to go

parole: promise to behave well ► **report(ing)**: present himself
weight (as of sth heavy) ► **settle**: come down and stay

lurking: lying in wait or ready to attack

worry: anxiety
I'll tell you straight (clearly, not trying to hide my meaning) ► **jail**: prison ► **an alert out...** (since he did not report to the
parole officer) ► **a favour** (in order to help me) ► **pretend**: act as if
go over: examine, study ► **with an open mind** (open to any
possibility) ► **I have a feeling** (the impression)
come up with: discover, find out

right; be right≠be wrong
hung up the phone: put back the receiver

she could not keep her eyes open (being so sleepy)
used to indicates sth that does not exist any more ► **apologetically** (as much as to say 'I'm sorry')
guest room (for friends... to sleep in) ► **second floor** (Am): first
floor (ground floor being first floor) ► **even so**: and yet
wailing: crying in a loud, usually high-pitched, voice
wakening; waken: make sb stop sleeping
bothering: worrying, annoying, upsetting
vital: essential

sleep, slept, slept
enjoyed: enjoy (a transitive verb!); enjoy sth: like sth

than toaster-waffles and the toaster hadn't worked for two days. As Brenda said, there was no use buying a new one when Donny Rubel could fix the old one good as new for ten dollars.

On that restless night, Clarence reflected that the real problem with retirement was you didn't have anything to do when you woke up and that meant you had nothing to talk about. Now Brenda's two sisters hung around the house so much he never could get a word in edgewise. They always cut him off when he began to talk.

At five in the morning as Brenda rumbled and snorted next to him, as far removed from his body on the double bed as she could be without falling off it, Clarence conceived his plan. Maybe it wasn't worth Donny's time to drive around for a ten-dollar job. But Clarence had worked up a solution. Once or twice, he hadn't had any cash when Donny fixed something, so he'd mailed a cheque to Donny. He had his address. Someplace in Howville. Timber Lane. That was it. Near those lakes where Clarence used to go swimming when he was a kid. Later in the morning, he'd find Donny's house, leave the toaster if Donny was out and a note saying he'd pick it up as soon as Donny had it ready.

Sleep made Clarence's eyelids begin to droop. He had a half-smile on his face as he dozed off. It was good to have a plan, to have something to do when you woke up.

Long before dawn, Kay heard the sounds of noisy activity in the living room. What was Donny doing? The thump of objects being dropped. Donny was packing. The inevitability of what those pulling and tugging sounds meant caused Kay to clamp her hands in fists over her mouth. If ever she needed to stay calm to keep him from becoming suspicious, it was in these next few hours. The only chance she had to escape him would be when he completed his final jobs and

waffle(s): flat cake marked with squares ▶ **... worked**: had been out of order ▶ **there was** (it was) **no use buying**: it was useless to ▶ **when**: considering that ▶ **fix... good as new**: mend it so well that it would be as good as a new one

restless≠calm, peaceful; to rest (after work) ▶ **reflected**: thought (carefully) ▶ **retirement**; retirement age: age when people usually stop working (retire)

hung around...: spent a lot of time in...

get a word in edgewise (Am) (edgeways): get a chance to speak ▶ **cut him off**: interrupted him

rumbled (making long low sounds) ▶ **snorted** (forcing air through her nose with a loud noise) ▶ **removed from**: away from **falling off it**; fall off a bicycle...

it wasn't worth...: it was useless coming here just for ten dollars

worked up: found (after spending time and effort) ▶ **once or twice**: on one or two occasions ▶ **so**: consequently

mailed (Am): sent by post

someplace (Am): somewhere ▶ Timber **Lane**: a lane is a narrow road in the country ▶ **go swimming**; go for a swim

out: not at home; Is John in? No, he's out

pick it up: come and get it (back) ▶ **had it ready**: had mended or repaired it

eyelids cover the eyes ▶ **droop**: hang down (through tiredness)

dozed off: fell asleep (partly or unintentionnally)

dawn: the first light of day, daybreak

thump: dull sound (not very clear) ▶ **packing** (bags... as if leaving) ▶ **tugging** (≠pulling) sounds made by objects

clamp (fasten) **her hands in fists** (hands when tightly closed)

stay calm: remain calm ▶ **keep** or prevent **from becoming suspicious**; to suspect ▶ **these next few hours**: the few hours which followed

completed; to complete: to finish doing

deliveries this morning. If he suspected anything, he would leave with her immediately.

She was able to pretend a drowsy smile when he handed her a cup of coffee at seven o'clock. 'You're so thoughtful, Donny,' she murmured as she sat up, again careful to tuck the blankets high under her arms.

He looked pleased. He was wearing dark-blue trousers and a short-sleeved white shirt. Instead of his usual sneakers he had on highly polished light-brown shoes. He had obviously taken special pains with his hair. It was plastered close to his skull as though he'd used hairspray. His mud-coloured eyes smouldered with excitement. 'I have it all figured out, Kay,' he told her. 'I'll pack most of the stuff in the van before I leave. That way, the minute I get back we can be married and have our wedding brunch. It has to be brunch because I don't want to wait until tonight. Then we'll just take off. I'm going to leave a message on the recorder right now that I'm on an extended vacation. I'll tell my best customers this morning that I'm getting married. That way, nobody will think it funny if we don't come back for a long time.'

He was obviously pleased with his plans. He bent over and kissed the top of Kay's head. 'Maybe when you have a baby, we'll go visit my mother. She always laughed at me when I told her I never got anywhere with girls. She used to say that the only way I'd ever get a girl was to tie her up. But when she sees how pretty you are and how much we love our baby, I bet she apologizes.'

He would not let Kay dress before breakfast. 'Just put on your robe.' The intensity in his body was approaching fever-pitch. She did not want to walk around in the sheer, clinging nightgown and robe.

'Donny, it's awfully chilly. Lend me your raincoat while we wait.'

He had left out a few utensils and the coffeepot, toaster, two plates. Everything else was packed. 'Most of the time we'll be staying in tents and cabins until

deliveries; to deliver: to take sth somewhere (to a customer)

to pretend... (although she did not feel like smiling) ▶ **drowsy**: feel drowsy, feel sleepy
thoughtful: kind, considerate ▶ **sat up** (with the back straight, upright) ▶ **tuck**: push
pleased: happy, glad ▶ **trousers** cover legs; (Am) pants
short-sleeved: with short sleeves (sleeves cover the arms)
highly: in a high degree, very ▶ **light-brown**≠dark-brown
taken special (great) **pains**: make a careful effort
plastered to: sticking to ▶ **close**: near ▶ **skull** (encloses the head) ▶ **hairspray** (to keep it in place) ▶ **smouldered**: burnt slowly (figuratively) ▶ **figured out**: thought about it all
stuff (fam): things
that way: like that ▶ **the minute I get back**: as soon as I get back

take off: leave, go away
right now: immediately ▶ **extended**: long, longer than usual
customers (who buy his services)
will think it funny (strange, odd): will be surprised

bent: moved the top part of his body downwards and forwards

we'll go visit (Am)**...** : we'll go <u>and</u> visit my mother
laughed at (mockingly) ▶ **I never got anywhere with girls**: I never formed relationships with girls
tie her up: fasten her (with chain, rope, string...)
I bet: I promise you, I'm sure
she apologizes: tells me she is sorry for what she said
he would not let Kay dress: he would not allow Kay to dress
robe (Am) (worn over your night clothes or after a bath)
fever-pitch; at fever-pitch: with a lot of excited feeling
sheer: vey thin and fine, almost transparent ▶ **clinging**: sticking to the body ▶ **awfully chilly**: very cold ▶ **lend me**: give me (temporarily)
he had left out: he had not packed

cabin(s): hut (in holiday camp)

we get to Wyoming, Kay. You like roughing it, don't you?'

She had to bite her lips to hold back shrieks of hysterical laughter. She had considered furnished condos, many of them very attractive, as 'roughing it'. Mike. Mike. The thought of his name changed the approaching laughter into a flood of tears. Don't, she warned herself, don't.

'Are you crying, Kay?' Donny leaned across the table and peered at her. Somehow she swallowed back the need to weep.

'Of course not.' She managed to sound breathless and teasing. 'Every bride gets the premarital jitters.'

The broad separation of his lips from his teeth was a caricature of a smile. 'Finish your breakfast, Kay. You've got to do your packing.'

He produced a bright-red suitcase. 'Surprise! I bought it for you.' But he refused to allow her to put on jeans and a T-shirt. 'No, Kay. Pack everything except your wedding dress.'

At nine-thirty he left, promising he wouldn't be gone more than two or three hours. In the living room his two old suitcases surrounded her new red one. Only the poster with them in the prom picture remained on the wall. 'We'll exchange our vows in front of it,' Donny had said.

The eyelet dress was too tight at the shoulders. It pulled and then tore as she reached deep into the springs of the couch for the screwdriver. Kay grasped the screwdriver in her hand, then laid it down and carefully shredded the scrap of paper on which Donny had written the marriage vows for her. He was going to kill her anyhow. She might as well defy him here where at least her body might someday be found and Mike would be free to stop looking for her.

With the calmness of desperation, she picked up the screwdriver, got up from the couch and walked to the metal plate, the heavy chain dragging with her. She crouched down, undid the already loosened screw,

Wyoming: a state in the North West ▶ **roughing it** (fam): living in conditions that are not very comfortable
hold back: control ▶ **shriek(s)**: very high, loud sound
furnished condo(s): flat with furniture in it

a flood of: a very large number of ▶ **she warned herself** (as of danger) ▶ **don't** (cry)

peered: looked carefully ▶ **swallowed back**: controlled, checked
weep, wept, wept: cry
sound breathless: seem as if she had difficulty in breathing
teasing: joking (flirtatiously) ▶ **have the jitters** (fam): feel very nervous (here before the wedding night) ▶ **broad**: wide, large

produced: showed, brought out ▶ **suitcase** (for packing things in)

he woudn't be gone: he wouldn't be absent

surrounded: were around
remained: were left, were still

too tight: not large enough
tore: got torn ▶ **reached** (her arms) **deep** (profoundly) **into the...**
for... (to get hold of the screwdriver) ▶ **grasped**: seized
laid it down: put it down
shredded: cut to shreds (small torn pieces) ▶ **scrap**: small piece (of paper, cloth)
anyhow: in any case
someday, some day: at a date in the future that is unknown
would be free to... (fam): could stop looking for her

dragging with her (slowly, heavily on the floor)
crouched down (bending her knees) ▶ **undid**: unfastened

dropped it onto the floor and put the head of the screw-driver into the second screw, the one that already had begun to loosen last evening.

Mike arrived at the O'Neil home at nine o'clock.

It was a beautiful June day, brilliant with sunlight. Incongruous that anything could be wrong on a day like this, Mike thought. As though in a dream, he saw a young man on the neighbouring lawn turn on a sprinkler. All around him, people were doing ordinary Saturday-morning chores, or going to play golf, or taking their kids on outings. For the last three hours, *he'd* been nailing more copies of Kay's picture to telephone poles around local swim clubs.

He rapped on the screen door, then let himself in. The others were already around the kitchen table. Virginia and Jack O'Neil, Jimmy Barrott, Virginia's three classmates. Mike was introduced to Marian Martin. He immediately sensed the additional tension in the room. Dreading to ask, he looked squarely at Jimmy Barrott. 'Tell me what you know.'

'We don't *know* anything,' Jimmy Barrott told him. 'We *think* Miss Martin may have spotted someone hiding on the path just when Kay was leaving the pic-nic. We're having that print blown up now. We're not even sure that it isn't a tree branch or something.' He hesitated as though he was about to go on, then said, 'I suggest we don't waste time. Let's keep on identi-fying the people in these pictures.'

Minutes passed. Mike sat helplessly. There wasn't any way he could help. He thought about driving to towns farther away that he hadn't yet covered with Kay's picture, but something held him here. He had the sense of time running out. He was sure everyone did.

At nine-thirty, Marian Martin shook her head impa-tiently. 'I thought I'd know every face, fool that I was. People change so. What I need is a list of the students who signed up for the reunion. That will help.'

head: the tip (extremity) of the 'blade' (≠handle)

to loosen: to get loose or free, to 'wobble'

sunlight or sunshine
wrong: undesirable, inconvenient
as though (as if he was) **in a dream**
neighbouring: nearby ▶ **lawn**: area of closely cut grass
sprinkler (to spray water on grass)
chore(s): job to keep a garden, a house... clean and tidy...
on outings (to the country, to the sea... for pleasure)
nailing: fastening with nails ▶ **copies**; copy: duplicate

rapped: knocked quickly, lightly ▶ **screen door** (Am): door outside the main door (for protection)

classmate(s): school friend (in the same year) ▶ **introduced**; the usual phrase is 'May I **introduce** you to Mrs so and so'
dread(ing): being afraid ▶ **squarely**; look at sb squarely in the eye

spotted: seen, noticed (from among many)

print: photograph ▶ **blown up**: enlarged; a blowup

about to go on (continue): on the point of going on
waste time (doing nothing...) ▶ **keep on**: go on, continue

helplessly: unable to help (the others and himself!)
he thought about...: he considered the idea of...
farther; further; far
held him here: made him stay here
of time running out: of time coming to an end, being used up
▶ **everyone did** (have that sense too)
shook her head, expressing impatience, disappointment...
fool: idiot; foolish, stupid, silly
change <u>so</u> (Am): change <u>so</u> much
signed up...: signed their names (intending to come to the reunion)

'It's Saturday,' Virginia said. 'The office is closed. But I'll call Gene Pearson at home. He lives four blocks from the school. He's the principal at Garden State,' she told Mike.

'I've met him.' Mike thought of Pearson's earlier reluctance.

But when he arrived a scant thirty minutes later, it was obvious that, like Jimmy Barrott, Gene Pearson had changed his attitude. He was unshaven; he looked as though he had thrown on the clothes nearest at hand; he apologized for taking so long.

Pearson handed the list of people who had attended the reunion to Marian. 'How can I help?' he said.

The phone rang. They all jumped. Virginia picked up the receiver. 'It's for you,' she told Jimmy Barrott.

Mike tried to decipher Jimmy's expression but could not. 'OK. Read him his stinking Miranda warnings and make sure he signs the statement,' Jimmy said. 'I'll be right down.'

The room was deathly quiet. Jimmy replaced the receiver and looked at Mike. 'We've been trying to track down a guy named Rudy Kluger who's just been released from prison. He served twenty years for murdering a girl whom he abducted from the picnic area near Garden State High.'

Mike's chest tightened as he waited.

Jimmy moistened his lips. 'This may have nothing to do with your wife's disappearance, but they just picked up Kluger in those same woods. He tried to waylay a young woman jogger.'

'And he may have been there on Wednesday,' Mike said.

'It's possible.'

'I'll go with you.' *Kay*, Mike thought, *Kay*.

As if suddenly feeling their task was hopeless, everyone at the table laid down the pictures. One of Virginia's classmates began to sob.

'Mike, Kay *did* phone you night before last,' Virginia reminded him.

office (of principal, here) ► **closed**: shut

meet, met, met ► **earlier**: dating back from earlier days
reluctance: unwillingness (to help); reluctant, disinclined
he: Pearson ► **a scant...**: hardly or barely thirty minutes

he was unshaven; to shave (with a razor)
thrown on: put on hurriedly, (too) rapidly ► (ready) **at hand**: near
in space ► **apologized** (said he was sorry) **for taking so long**
(in coming) ► **attended**: were present at

jumped: made a quick sudden movement (in surprise...)

decipher: find the meaning of
stinking: damned ► **Miranda warnings** (Am) established by
Supreme Court concerning arrested people ► **statement**: official
document 'stating' these warnings ► **I'll be right down**: I'm coming right now ► **deathly quiet**: absolutely silent (suggesting
death)
track down: find (murderers...) ► **named**; to name
served twenty years: spent twenty years in prison
abducted: took away illegally, using force or deception

Mike's chest tightened: he was oppressed by worry
moistened his lips (with his tongue); moist: slightly wet
have nothing to do with: be without any connection with
picked up: caught
a woman jogger: notice the way this is put (a lady doctor...)
he may have been there: perhaps he was there

Mike thought: Mike thought to himself (hence the italics)
task: (piece of) work, job ► **hopeless**: led nowhere
laid down the pictures (as if giving up)
sob: cry noisily, breathing in short breaths
did (in fact) **phone** ► **night before last**: the night before the last one
(last but one) ► **reminded him** (of it): made him remember it

'But not last night. And now Kluger is trying to pick up someone else.'

Mike walked behind Jimmy Barrott to the car. He was aware that he must be having a shock reaction. He felt absolutely nothing, not pain nor sorrow nor anger. Again he whispered Kay's name but it evoked no emotion.

Jimmy Barrott was backing the car from the driveway when Jack O'Neil dashed out of the house. 'Hold it!' he shouted. 'Your office is on the phone. A woman named Vina Howard saw one of those posters with Kay's picture and swears Kay was in her dress shop in Pleasantwood yesterday afternoon.'

Jimmy Barrott slammed on the brakes. He and Mike jumped from the car and rushed into the house. Jimmy grabbed the phone. Mike and the others crowded around him. Jimmy asked questions and barked instructions. He hung up and addressed Mike.

'This Howard woman and her assistant both swear it was Kay. She was with some guy in his twenties. The Howard woman thought they were high on something, but after she talked to my people, she realized Kay was probably terrified. Kay scratched the letter *H* on the wall in the dressing room.'

'A guy in his *twenties*,' Mike exclaimed. 'That means it can't be Kluger.' Relief mingled with new dread. 'She tried to write something in the dressing room.' His voice choked as he whispered, 'A word starting with *H*...'

'She might have been trying to write HELP,' Jimmy Barrott snapped. 'The point is at least we know she wasn't with Kluger.'

'But what was she doing in a dress shop?' Jack O'Neil asked.

Jimmy Barrott's face registered disbelief. 'I know it sounds crazy, but she was buying a wedding dress.'

'I've got to talk to that woman,' Mike said.

'She and her assistant are going to be here as fast as a squad car can deliver them,' Jimmy Barrott told him.

pick up: choose (as his victim)
someone else: another girl; something else, somewhere else
he was aware: he realized

sorrow: feeling of deep sadness ▶ **anger**; angry
whispered: murmured; a whisper

backing the car: driving backwards
dashed out: rushed out ▶ **hold it**: stop, wait
shouted (in a loud voice, loudly)

swears: says very firmly, very seriously; swear, swore, sworn

slammed...: hurriedly pressed on the **brakes** (brakes are used
to reduce speed) ▶ **jumped...**: got out of the car quickly
grabbed (impatiently) ▶ **crowded**: gathered, assembled
barked (in a loud rough voice) (a dog barks)

high on something (fam): on drugs, 'spacey'
my people: people working under me
scratched: wrote by scratching with the straight pin (p 78)

Mike exclaimed: no reflexive pronoun!
relief: ease given by reduction of anxiety ▶ **mingled**: mixed
dread: great fear, terror
choked: was suffocating
starting with, beginning with: notice the prepositions!

snapped (annoyingly): said in a sharp voice ▶ **the point**: the
essential thing

registered: showed (by his expression) ▶ **disbelief**: inability to
believe ▶ **it sounds crazy**: it seems mad (to say)
I've got to talk: I must talk

squad: section of a police force ▶ **deliver them**: bring them

He pointed to the table. 'There's a good chance they can pick out the guy your wife was with from those pictures.'

Clarence Gerber was astonished to see the change in the way things looked on the approach to Howville. In his day, it had been really rustic, with mountains and the hidden lakes. It never developed like most of the towns around. Pollution had set in years ago. Waste from factories had wrecked the swimming and fishing. But he wasn't prepared for the absolute desolation of the area. Houses were rotting away like they'd been abandoned for ever. Junk and wrecked cars were piles of rust in the gullies off the road. Wonder why a fellow like Donny Rubel would stick himself out here? Clarence thought.

Memories long buried came back to him. Timber Lane wasn't directly off the highway. He should take that fork down the road a mile or two, go about five miles, then make a right on a dirt road that turned into Timber Lane.

Clarence was pleased with the sunny day, pleased that his eleven-year-old car was behaving so well. He'd just had the oil changed and even though it puffed a little on hills, 'Just like me,' he'd say, it was a good heavy automobile. Not like the pieces of tin they call cars today and stick with price tags that in his day would have bought a mansion.

Brenda's sisters had arrived before he'd even had a cup of coffee. They all were glad to see him on his way, all full of the talk of that fellow who was nailing pictures of his missing wife all over the county. Clarence tried to picture Brenda missing. He chuckled. They'd never sue him for disturbing the peace hammering her picture around.

He found the fork in the road. Stay to the right, he told himself. The sign for Timber Lane might be gone, but he'd know it when he saw it. The toaster was beside him on the seat. He'd remembered to bring a

pick out: see clearly among others, recognize, 'spot'

looked: seemed ▶ **on the approach...**: as he approached... ▶ **in his day**: when he was young(er) ▶ **rustic**: typical of the country
hidden (by the woods) ▶ **developed** (with building, industry)
set in: begun ▶ **waste**: unwanted materials
factories; factory, firm, plant ▶ **wrecked**: ruined

rotting away (into ruins) ▶ **like they'd been** (Am): as if
junk: old or unwanted objects ▶ **wrecked**: badly damaged
rust (formed on wet metal) ▶ **gullies**: narrow valleys ▶ **off**: at a distance from ▶ (I) **wonder** (ask myself) ▶ **stick himself out here** (fam): come and live, stay, settle here
memories: things you remember ▶ **buried**: forgotten
not directly off the highway: some distance away from
fork: junction ▶ **go**: (here) drive
make a right (fam): turn right ▶ **dirt road**: rough country road made of earth or gravel

behaving well (as if it was a person!): running well
he had the oil changed (by the mechanic) ▶ **puffed**: breathed with difficulty, so to speak ▶ going up **hills** (lower than mountains)
automobile (Am) ▶ **tin**: soft white metal; sardine tin
(on which) **they stick tags** (small tickets showing the price)
mansion: large impressive-looking house

glad: pleased, happy, delighted ▶ **on his way**: leaving
full of the talk: talking exclusively about
all over the county: throughout the county
picture: imagine ▶ **chuckled**: laughed quietly
sue: take legal action against ▶ **disturb(ing)** the peace: annoy people in a public place ▶ (by) **hammering** (here): hitting nails into phone poles (with a hammer)
(road) **sign** ▶ **might be gone**: might have disappeared
know: recognize

blank sheet of paper and an envelope. If Donny wasn't home, he'd write a note. Maybe when he came back to pick up the toaster, Donny and he could have a nice visit. Donny sure must get lonely living around here. Didn't seem like there was a soul for miles around.

The second screw was on the floor. The third one was beginning to work loose. Kay rotated her weight from side to side as she turned the handle of the screwdriver. She sensed some slack developing in it. Oh God, please don't let it break. How long had he been gone? At least an hour? The phone had rung twice and the caller received the message about the extended vacation, but Donny did not call. She straightened up and brushed the perspiration from her forehead. A light-headedness warned her that she was nearing exhaustion. Her legs were cramped. Hating to waste the time, she stood up and stretched. She turned and her glance fell on the prom photo on the opposite wall. Sickened, she dropped back into the crouch and with a new burst of energy twisted the handle of the screwdriver. Suddenly it was twirling in her hand. The third screw was free. She pulled it out and for the first time dared to hope that she might really have a chance.

And then she heard it, the sound of a car, the squeal of brakes. No, no, no. Numbly she laid the screwdriver on the floor and folded her hands. Let him see what she was doing. Let him kill her here and now.

At first she thought she was fantasizing. It couldn't be. But it was. Somebody was thumping on the door. An old man's voice was calling, 'Hey, anybody home?'

The wailing of the siren in the squad car, the mad dash through red lights made the ten-mile ride from Pleasant-wood to the O'Neil home in Jefferson Township seem an eternity to Vina Howard and her assistant, Edna. *I saw that woman's picture last night, Vina reproached herself silently, and all I worried about was that wall-*

blank sheet of paper: a piece... with nothing written on it
note: short informal letter; note paper
pick up: get back, collect ► **have a nice visit** (talk...)
sure (Am): surely ► **lonely**: unhappy because he is alone
(it) **didn't seem** ► **like** there was (Am) **a soul**: as if there was anybody living... (any human being)
'one' is used to avoid the repetition of 'screw'
work loose: be free, unfastened ► the **weight** of her body
handle: part of a tool which you hold in your hand
slack: looseness (the screwdriver did not seem to work as efficiently)

caller: sb making a telephone call
straightened up: rose to a standing position with the back straight ► **brushed**: removed with her hand ► **light-headed-(ness)**: mentally disoriented ► **nearing exhaustion**: getting near to fatigue ► **cramped**: contracted ► **hating**: really not wanting
stretched: put her arms or legs out straight ► **glance**: quick look
sickened: shocked and angry
dropped... crouch (close to the floor) ► **burst...**: short violent effort ► **twisted**: turned
twirling: turning quickly and lightly round and round

a chance (to escape)
squeal: long high-pitched sound
numbly (as if no longer capable of thinking or acting)
folded her hands: crossed them over her chest (upper part of body) ► **here and now** (emphatic): at the present time, rather than in the future ► **fantasizing**: imagining sth pleasant happening ► **thumping**: knocking very hard
calling: crying ► (is there) **anybody** (at) **home**?

wailing: loud high-pitched sound ► **mad dash**: frantic, very quick drive **through** (ignoring) **red** (traffic) **lights** ► **ride**: journey (by car...)

paper. If only... It should have been obvious that there
was something wrong. That fellow was in such a hurry.
She insisted on trying on the dress, tried to stall by
asking for other dresses. He opened the curtain of the
dressing area as though he didn't trust her. And all I
thought about was wallpaper.

Jimmy Barrott cut Vina off when she tried to tell all
this at the O'Neil home. 'Mrs Howard, please. We
believe that whoever abducted Kay Crandell may be in
these pictures. Won't you study them now? You're
sure he had red hair? Sure he had blue eyes?'

'Absolutely,' Vina said. 'In fact, didn't we comment
that he looked as though he'd just had his hair set?'

Marian Martin got up from the table. 'Sit here. I
want to go over the list again.' The terrible gnawing
feeling that she had missed something–why was it
exploding inside her? She walked into the recreation
room. Gene Pearson followed her.

Virginia beckoned to her friends. They clustered on
a semi-circular couch across the room from Marian
Martin and Gene Pearson.

Mike stood at the table watching the earnest faces
of the two middle-aged women who had seen Kay yesterday. Pleasantwood. He had been there. 'What time
did you say Kay was in your shop?' he asked Vina.

'Around three o'clock. Maybe quarter past or so.'

He had left this house yesterday at three o'clock and
driven directly to Pleasantwood. He must have been in
that town when Kay was there. The irony made him
want to smash the wall with his fists.

Jack O'Neil was stacking the prints after Vina and
Edna rejected them. 'You couldn't miss him,' Vina
told Jimmy Barrott. 'All you have to do is look for that
head of hair.' She paused and picked up one picture.
'You know, it's funny. There's something about this
one...'

'What is?' Jimmy Barrott snapped.

'There's something so familiar.' Vina bit her lip in
irritation. 'Oh, I'm wasting time. I know what it is. I'm

obvious (at first glance), evident
something wrong (that should make her suspicious) ▶ **hurry**: wish to get sth done quickly ▶ **to stall**: to play for time, to delay deliberately
trust: place confidence in

cut Vina off: interrupted Vina

believe: think ▶ **whoever**: the person who ▶ **abducted**: carried off illegally
red (of hair): of a reddish-brown colour
comment that: say that, remark that
he looked as though: he gave the impression that ▶ **set**: fixed in desired style
go over: study, examine ▶ **gnawing**: tormenting
she had missed something: she had not seen or noticed sth
recreation room (Am)(for games, relaxation, etc.)

beckoned: made a sign (to ask them to come) ▶ **clustered**: gathered ▶ **across**: on the other side of

earnest: showing serious feeling or intention
middle-aged: aged between 45 and 60 (approximately)

around: at about ▶ (a) **quarter past** (three) **or so** (or sth like that, approximately, roughly)

smash: hit, strike very hard ▶ **fist(s)**: hand when tightly closed
stack(ing): make into a stack or pile
you couldn't miss him (he is so easy to recognize)
look for (try to find) **that head of hair** (the hair on the head, when copious) ▶ **paused**: stopped speaking ▶ **picked up**: took
funny: strange

snapped: said quickly in an angry or annoyed way
familiar; be familiar with: know well ▶ **bit** (with her teeth)

looking at *his* picture.' She pointed into the den where Gene Pearson was going over the reunion list with Marian.

Edna took the picture from her. 'I see what you mean, but...' her voice trailed off. She continued to study the picture. 'It sounds silly,' she said, 'but there's something about this man with the beard and dark glasses...'

In the den, Marian Martin was studying the list of alumni from a different viewpoint. She was searching for a name that for some reason she'd let slip by. She was just beginning to read the *R* list when something that Virginia was saying caught her attention.

'Remember how we all wanted to dress like Kay Wesley? She could have been prom queen when she chaperoned our prom.'

The prom, Marian Martin thought. That's what I've been trying to remember. Donny Rubel, that odd, withdrawn boy who had such a crush on Kay. Her fingers raced down the page. He had signed up for the reunion, but she absolutely had not seen him in any of the pictures. That was why his name hadn't jumped out at her.

'Virginia,' she asked, 'did any of you see Donny Rubel at the reunion?'

Virginia looked at her classmates. 'I didn't see him,' she said slowly. The others nodded in agreement. 'I've heard he has some kind of fix-it business, but he was always a loner,' Virginia continued. 'I doubt if he bothered with anyone from school after we graduated. I think I'd have noticed him if he showed up for the reunion.'

'Donny Rubel,' Gene Pearson interrupted. 'I'm *sure* I spoke to him. He even talked about his fix-it business. I asked if he'd speak on career day. It was right at the end of the picnic. He was in such a rush, he brushed me off.'

'A little heavyset,' Marian snapped. 'Dark-brown hair, brown eyes. Just under six feet tall.'

den: comfortable, usually secluded (isolated) room

trailed off: became gradually quieter and then stopped
silly: stupid

viewpoint: point of view, standpoint ▶ **searching for**: trying very
hard to find ▶ **let slip by**: missed, failed to see
the *R* list: the list of names beginning with R
caught her attention or drew or attracted her attention
(do you) remember? ▶ **dress like**: wear the same clothes as
prom (beauty) **queen**
chaperoned our prom: acted as a chaperon at our dance (to
ensure proper behaviour)
withdrawn: introvert, unsociable
had such a crush <u>on</u> Kay; crush: uncontrollable feeling of love
for ▶ **raced** (moved very quickly) **down the page**

jumped out at her; sth jumps out at you, it is extremely easy to
notice

nodded in agreement: moved their heads downwards to
express their agreement ▶ **I've heard** (it said that)
a loner prefers to be alone rather than with a group of people
bothered with: was interested in, cared about
showed up (fam): came, turned up (fam)

if he'd (would accept to) **speak** ▶ **right at the end**: at the very
end ▶ **in such a rush**: in such a hurry
brushed me off: refused to talk to me
heavyset: with a large solid body
under: less than ▶ **six feet**: 1.82 m

'No. This guy was pretty skinny. He had a beard and damn little hair. In fact I was surprised when he said he graduated only eight years ago. Wait a minute.' Gene Pearson stood up, and ran a hand over the stubble of beard on his face. 'He's in one of those pictures with me. Let me get it.'

As one, Pearson, Marian Martin, Virginia and her classmates raced from the den into the kitchen. Vina Howard had just grabbed the picture of Pearson and Donny Rubel from her assistant's hand.

'He wore a wig,' Vina shrieked.

'That's why we thought his hair looked so set. That's the man who came into my shop.'

Marian Martin, Virginia and her friends stared at the thin, bearded stranger whom none of them had recognized. But Gene Pearson was shouting, 'That's Rubel. That's Rubel.'

Jimmy Barrott grabbed the list from Marian's hand. Donny Rubel's address was next to his name. 'Timber Lane. Howville,' he said. 'That's about fifteen miles from here. The squad car is outside,' he told Mike. 'Let's go.'

Clarence Gerber could not believe his ears. A woman's voice inside the house kept shouting at him to go for help, to phone the police, to tell them she was Kay Crandell. But suppose this was some kind of joke or whoever was in there was on drugs or something. Clarence decided to try to take a look inside. But it was impossible to force the doors or shutters open.

'Don't waste time,' Kay shouted. 'He'll be back any minute. Go for help. He'll kill you if he finds you here.'

Clarence gave one last pull at the shutter on the front window. It was bolted from the inside. 'Kay Crandell,' he said aloud, now realizing why the name was familiar. That was the woman Brenda and her sisters were talking about this morning, the one whose husband was putting up posters. He'd better get to the police fast.

skinny (fam): very thin (unattractively)
damn (fam): very

ran a hand: moved a hand lightly along ▶ **stubble of beard**: short hairs on his face (since he did not shave)

as one: as one man (they all raced at the same time)
raced: rushed, dashed
grabbed: suddenly taken hold of (showing her impatience)

shrieked: made a very high loud sound (because she was excited)

bearded: wearing a beard ▶ **stranger**: sb they did not know
shouting (expressing excitement too)

was next to: came just after
mile(s): 1.609 km; 5 miles = 8 km (approximately)
outside≠inside (adverbs here)

could not believe his ears: was very surprised by what he heard
kept shouting at him: repeatedly shouted at him ▶ **go <u>for</u> help**: go and get some help
kind: sort ▶ **joke**: sth intended to be funny (jocular)
whoever: the person who, anybody
take a look: look
force the doors... open: use physical force to open
any minute (now): at any minute, in no time
finds; find, found, found≠lose, lost, lost

to give **a pull**: to pull ▶ **front window**≠back window
bolted: locked with a bolt (a metal bar)
familiar (to him): known to him

putting up posters: fixing posters in a place where they will be seen

Totally forgetting the toaster he had set down on the porch, Clarence got back in his car and tried to coax speed from the aging engine as it wheezed and groaned up the twisting, bumpy dirt road.

Kay heard the car pull away. *Let him be in time, let him be in time.* How far was it to a phone? How long would it be before the police would get here? Ten minutes? Fifteen? Half an hour? It might be too late. The fourth screw was still tightly in place. She could never work it free. But maybe. With three screws missing, she was able to use the screwdriver to force a corner of the metal plate away from the wall. She began to work the chain into the opening until she could grasp it in both hands. She arched her back, straightened her arms and dragged the chain with her until she was rewarded by a crunching, ripping sound, then she toppled backward as the metal plate separated from the wall, a chunk of aging plaster still clinging to it.

Kay stood up, feeling the thin trickle of blood where her head had grazed a corner of the couch. The metal plate was heavy. She grasped it under one arm, looped the chain around her wrist and started for the door. The familiar sound of the van driving into the clearing assaulted her ears.

The excitement building in Donny had reached fever pitch. He'd gotten rid of every single job. He'd explained to all his customers that he was getting married and taking a long vacation. They'd looked surprised, then said how pleased they were for him and they'd sure miss him. Said let us know when you come back.

He'd never come back. Everywhere he went, he kept seeing Kay's pictures. Mike Crandell was looking all over for her. Donny felt for the gun in the inside pocket of his jacket. He'd kill Mike and Kay and himself before he'd lose her.

But he didn't want to think about that. It was going to be fine. He had taken care of everything. He and

set down: put down; set, set, set
porch (Am): veranda ► **coax speed...**: gently persuaded his old car to run fast ► **groaned**: made a long deep sound (as in pain)
bumpy, uneven (full of bumps)≠flat
pull away: move away, leave
how long...?: how much time would it take the police **to get here** (to arrive here)?

'still' expresses continuation ► **tightly**: firmly
work it free (loose): unfasten ► **missing** (off the plate)
force... away: take away (using physical force)

opening: space through which objects can pass
she arched her back (into the shape of an arch)
straightened: made straight ► **dragged**: drew along with force
rewarded (in return for her effort) ► **crunching** (as of sth crushed between teeth) ► **ripping** (as of sth torn apart) ► **toppled** (fell)
backward(s) ► **chunk**: thick solid piece broken off the wall ► **clinging to it**: attached to the plate
trickle of blood (flowing in very small quantity)
grazed: touched lightly in passing, brushed
looped the chain: curved... (the ends crossing); a plane makes a loop ► **for**: towards, in the direction of

assaulted her ears; an assault, an attack

building (up): becoming more intense ► **had reached** (attained)
fever pitch (a very high level of excitement) ► **he had gotten** (Am for 'got') **rid of**: he had finished ► **every single job**: every job without exception
pleased: happy; pleased <u>with</u> sth or sb ► **they'd sure** (Am for surely) **miss him** ► (They) **said**...
kept seeing pictures: saw pictures all the time
looking all over for her: trying to find her everywhere
felt for: tried to find (by touch) ► **inside pocket**; inside pages (of a newspaper)
think <u>about</u> that: notice the preposition; also think <u>of</u> ► **fine**: ok, perfect ► **he had taken care of everything**: he had planned everything

Kay would get married in a few minutes and have their wedding brunch. He'd bought champagne and some stuff from the deli and a coconut cake that looked a little like a wedding cake. Then they'd go away. By tonight they'd be in Pennsylvania. He knew some good camping grounds. He fretted that he hadn't had time to buy a wedding nightgown for Kay. But the one she'd been wearing was real pretty.

He reached the fork in the road. Another ten minutes. He hoped Kay had memorized the wedding service. A June bride. He wished he'd thought of buying her flowers. He'd make it up to her. 'Your husband will take care of you, Kay,' he said aloud. The sun was so bright that even with the dark glasses he began to squint. Happy is the bride that the sun shines on today. He thought of Kay's sun-streaked hair. Tonight her head would be lying on his shoulder. Her arms would be around him. She'd be telling him how much she loved him.

He heard before he saw the old car approaching. He had to pull to one side to let it pass. He got a glimpse of straggly white hair, of some skinny little guy bent over the wheel. He had posted big No Trespassing signs at the last bend on the road to his place and anyhow nobody would bother going near a boarded-up house. Even so, Donny felt his body tingle with anger. He didn't want people snooping around.

Recklessly he pressed his foot on the accelerator. The van bounced along the twisting road. Straggly white hair. That car. He'd seen it before. As he brought the van to a halt, Donny remembered yesterday's phone call. *Clarence Gerber.* That was the guy in the car.

He jumped out of the van and started to run towards the house, then saw the toaster on the porch. He remembered the intense way Gerber was driving, like he was trying to make the car go faster. *Gerber was going for the police.*

Donny jumped back into the van. He'd catch up with

stuff (fam): things ▶ **deli**(catessen): shop that sells high quality foods imported from other countries ▶ **wedding cake** (often with several levels) ▶ **Pennsylvania**: a state in the North East
camping ground(s), campsite ▶ **he fretted that**: he worried about the fact that
real(ly) **pretty**: adjectives are often used as adverbs in American
reached the fork: came as far as the junction

bride: woman on her wedding day (or newly married)
make it up to her: compensate her for not buying flowers

bright; the sun shines bright
squint: look with eyes partly shut ▶ **the bride** on whom **the sun shines** ▶ **sun-streaked**: made bright(er) in places by the sun (p 15)

pull (move) **to one side** ▶ **glimpse**: short and not very clear view
straggly, straggling: growing in different directions
(steering) **wheel** ▶ **posted**: put up (signs) ▶ **trespass(ing)**: enter sb's property without permission ▶ **bend**: curve, turn
(leading) **to** ▶ **place**: home ▶ **boarded-up**: closed with wooden boards, bars... ▶ **even so**: however ▶ **tingle**: feel an uncomfortable feeling (on the skin...) ▶ **snooping** (fam): secretly looking around to find out things ▶ **recklessly**: not caring about danger
bounced (up and down)
he brought the van to a halt: made it stop moving; bring, brought, brought
guy (Am, fam): fellow, chap, man

jumped (quickly) **out of the van**

the intense way or manner (in which) **Gerber was driving** ▶ **like he was trying** (Am): as if he was trying
going for the police (to report to the police)
catch up with him: reach him on the road by driving faster

Gerber. That old wreck he was driving couldn't go more than forty miles an hour. He'd run him off the road. And then... Donny started the van, his mouth a thin, unforgiving line. And then he'd come back here and take care of Kay, who he knew now had betrayed him.

Mike sat beside Jimmy Barrott in the back of the squad car, listening as the siren wailed and screeched. Kay is fifteen miles away, twelve miles away, eight miles away. Oh God, please, if You exist and I know You do, anything You want of me, I swear I'll do it. Please. Please, he thought.

The landscape had changed sharply. Suddenly they were no longer in pretty, suburban towns with well-kept lawns and budding rose bushes. The highway was surrounded by junk-filled gullies. The traffic had almost disappeared.

Jimmy Barrott was studying a county road map. 'I bet there hasn't been a street sign around here for twenty years,' he muttered. 'We'll hit a fork in the road in about a mile,' he barked to the patrolman at the wheel. 'Veer to the right.'

They were almost at the fork when the driver jammed on the brakes to avoid hitting an old man who was swaying in the middle of the road, whose blood-encrusted hair clung to his head. In the gully below they could see a car burst into flames. Jimmy flung open the door, jumped out and lifted the old man into the squad car.

Clarence Gerber gasped, 'He ran me off the road. Donny Rubel. He's got Kay Crandell.'

With total disbelief, Kay heard the screeching of the tires as the van roared up the road. Donny must have seen the car the old man was driving, must have suspected something. Don't let Donny hurt him, she pleaded to a God who seemed silent and far away. She hobbled to the door, pushed back the bolts,

old wreck: dilapidated old car ('wheezing, groaning'), 'melon'

an hour: per hour ► **run him off the road**: force him to leave the road ► **started the van** (with the ignition key)

unforgiving: unwilling to forgive, pitiless, cruel

betrayed him: was false or disloyal to him

screeched: gave a loud piercing sound

I swear I'll do it: I (solemnly) promise I'll do it

landscape: rural scenery, countryside ► **sharply**: clearly, distinctly, 'suddenly' ► **well-kept**: neat and clean

budding; bud: flower before it opens ► **rose <u>bush(es)</u>**, not tree(s)! ► **filled** with **junk**: full of unwanted objects ► **gullies**; gully, small valley

county: division of a state ► a **map** shows where the roads are

I bet (that): I am certain that ► **street sign**: road sign

muttered (in a low voice, annoyingly) ► **hit** (fam): arrive at

patrolman (Am): policeman ► **at the wheel**: driving

veer: change direction suddenly

jammed...: put his foot down hard on...

avoid hitting: in order not to crash into

swaying: moving slowly from one side to another

clung to (as if stuck to) ► **below**: farther down

burst into flames: suddenly start to burn very strongly ► **flung open the door**: quickly opened the door ► **lifted the old man** (up) **into the squad car**

gasped: said, taking short quick breaths (of air)

...he's got Kay Crandell (Gerber can't say more, being shocked and out of breath)

disbelief: inability to believe; to disbelieve: not to believe

roared up...: went up the road, making a very loud noise

hurt: cause injury or pain (as in an accident)

pleaded: asked imploringly, 'begged'

hobbled: walked with difficulty ► **bolt(s)**: metal bar(s)

yanked the door open. If that old man was able to make it to the phone, she had a chance. She might be able to hide in the woods until help came. There was no use trying to run away. She could hardly move with the weight she was dragging. Some instinct made her pull the door closed behind her. If Donny searched the house it would give her a few additional minutes.

Where should she try to hide? The brilliant sun was high in the sky, mercilessly finding its way into every opening between the branches of the shaggy, over-grown trees. He would be sure that she'd try for the road. She stumbled towards the woods on the other side of the clearing and headed for a cluster of maple trees. She had barely reached them when the van roar-ed back up the road and stopped. She watched as, gun drawn, Donny walked with deliberate, precise steps towards the house.

'Trust me. I know where I'm going,' Clarence Gerber told Jimmy Barrott, his voice uneven and quivering. 'I was there five minutes ago.'

'The map says...' Jimmy Barrott clearly thought that Gerber was confused.

'Forget the map,' Mike ordered. 'Do it his way.'

'It's kind of a shortcut,' Clarence told them. It was hard to talk. He was feeling kind of dizzy. He could hardly believe it had happened. One minute he was driving, fast as he could push his good old car, the next he was being cut off, was being forced to the right. He'd barely had a glimpse of Donny Rubel's van before he'd felt his wheels go off the road. Any other car and he'd have been killed. But he'd hung onto the wheel for dear life until the car stopped turning over. He'd smelled the gas and knew he had to get out fast. The driver's door was pinned to the ground, but he'd managed to push open the passenger door and then climb up the gully. 'Down here,' he told the driver. 'Listen to me, will you? Now that next right, by the

yanked open: opened suddenly and forcefully ▶ **make it to...**: go to

to hide, hid, hidden (no reflexive pronoun!) ▶ **there was no use trying**: it was not worth trying

(heavy) **weight**; to weigh (no 't'!) ▶ **pull the door closed**: close it by pulling ▶ **searched**: spent time looking for her in the house

mercilessly: pitilessly ▶ **finding...**: filtering through

opening: space ▶ **shaggy**: covered with (too) thick vegetation ▶ **overgrown**: (too) big ▶ **try for**: try to go towards

stumbled (walked with difficulty, almost falling)

headed for: moved towards ▶ **cluster**: small group ▶ **maple tree(s)**: *érable* ▶ **barely**: hardly, scarcely

gun drawn (out, in hand) ▶ **deliberate**: slow and careful

trust me: have trust (confidence) in me

uneven: not regular, varying ▶ **quivering**: trembling slightly

clearly: obviously

confused: unable to think clearly

forget (here): ignore ▶ **his way**: the way he wants

kind of (Am) is used to avoid giving details ▶ **shortcut**: quicker way of going there ▶ **kind of** (Am): slightly ▶ **dizzy** (as if everything was spinning, turning round)

(as) **fast as** ▶ **the next** (minute): the following minute

cut off: made unable to go on ▶ **forced** (to go) **to the right**

a **glimpse**: a brief incomplete view; catch a glimpse of

felt (realized that **his wheels** were going **off** (leaving) **the road** (if he had had) **any other car** ▶ **he'd hung onto**: held tightly

for dear life: with the greatest possible effort ▶ **turning over**: rolling over ▶ **gas(oline)** (Am): petrol

pinned to: as if fastened to

climb up (by effort, using hands and feet)

that next right: the next turn on the right ▶ **by**: near

No Trespassing sign. His place is in a clearing a couple of hundred yards down.'

Mike watched as Jimmy Barrott and the policemen drew their guns. *Kay, be there for me, be there. Be alive. Please.* The squad car burst into the clearing and came to a stop behind Donny Rubel's fix-it van.

Kay watched as Donny opened the door and kicked it aside. She could almost feel his fury when he realized she was gone. The cabin was less than thirty yards from the clump of trees where she was hiding. Let him start looking on the road, she begged.

An instant later, he was framed in the doorway, looking around wildly, the gun pointed straight in front of him. She hugged her arms against her sides. If he ever looked this way, the white eyelet dress would show through the leaves and branches. Any movement would cause the chain to rattle.

She heard the sound of the approaching vehicle at the same moment she saw Donny jump back into the house. But he did not close the door. Instead he stood, waiting. The car pulled in behind the van. Kay saw the flashing red dome. A police car. Be careful, she thought, be careful. He doesn't care whom he kills. She watched as two uniformed policemen emerged from the car. They had parked on the side of the cabin. The windows were boarded up. There was no way they could see Donny, who was now stepping out onto the porch, a reckless caricature of a smile on his face. The back door of the squad car opened. Two men got out. *Mike. Mike was here.* The policemen had drawn their guns. They were moving cautiously against the side of the house. Mike was with them. Donny was tiptoeing across the porch. He would shoot when they turned the corner. He didn't care if he died. *He would kill Mike!*

The clearing was utterly still. Even the squawks of the bluejays and the buzzing of the flies had stopped. Kay had a fleeting sense of the ending of the world. Mike had moved forward. He was only a few feet from the corner of the porch where Donny waited.

place (fam): a person's home; come to my place
yard(s): 3 feet (91.44 cm)

drew their guns (out ready to fire); draw, drew, drawn
alive: living ▶ **burst into...**: entered suddenly and with great force
came to a stop: stopped

kicked it aside (to one side, with his foot)

clump: group of trees growing close together
begged: asked in an anxious way, 'pleaded'
framed (like a picture in a frame) ▶ **doorway**: space where a door opens into a room ▶ **wildly**: in a very excited way
hugged: held tightly
this way: in this direction ▶ **show**: be visible

rattle: shake, with quick repeated knocking noises

jump back into: enter suddenly and quickly
instead (of closing the door); instead of: in lieu of
pulled in: arrived, slowing down to a stop ▶ **flashing**: shining suddenly and brightly for a short time
he doesn't care... (it is of no importance to him, it does not worry him)
there was no way...: they could not possibly see...
stepped out: walked out
reckless: showing he did not care about the possible bad or dangerous results of his actions ▶ **opened**: no reflexive pronoun!

cautiously: with caution, not taking any risks
tiptoeing: walking quietly on the toes (five digits of foot)
shoot: fire a bullet (from gun); shoot, shot, shot

utterly still: perfectly silent ▶ **squawk(s)**: loud sharp angry cry
bluejay(s): jay(bird) ▶ **buzzing**: continuous sound ▶ **flies**; fly: *mouche* ▶ **fleeting**: brief, passing, swift

Kay stepped from behind the tree. 'I'm here, Donny,' she called.

She saw him running towards her, tried to press against the tree, felt the bullet graze her forehead, heard the sound of other guns exploding, saw Donny crumple onto the ground. Then Mike was running towards her. Sobbing with joy, Kay stumbled towards the clearing, and into the arms that were rushing to enfold her.

Jimmy Barrott was not a sentimental man, but his eyes were suspiciously moist as he watched Kay and Mike, silhouetted against the trees, holding each other as if they'd never let go.

One of the policemen was bending over Donny Rubel. 'He's gone,' he told Jimmy.

The other cop had wrapped a bandage around Clarence Gerber's head. 'You're a tough one,' he told Clarence. 'Mostly lacerations as far as I can see. We'll get you to a hospital.'

Clarence was absorbing every detail to tell Brenda and her sisters. The way Kay Crandell had tried to draw Donny Rubel's fire, the way Donny had run towards her, shooting at her. The way that young couple was holding on to each other, now crying in each other's arms. He looked around so that later he could describe the cabin. The women would want to know every detail. His glance spotted something on the porch and he hurried over to claim it. Even though he was a hero, it would be just like Brenda to remind him that he had forgotten to bring the toaster home.

stepped; to step, to take a step (forward, backward...)
call(ed): say sth loudly to attract attention

graze: touch lightly while passing, brush against
exploding: making a very loud noise
crumple: fall in an uncontrolled way
sob(bing): cry noisily, drawing in breath of air frequently

enfold: hold closely, in a very gentle, loving way

suspiciously: (here) surprisingly ▶ **moist**: slightly wet (with tears)
silhouetted against: seen against a dark background (of trees)
let go: stop holding each other
bending over: leaning over; bend, bent, bent
he's gone: he <u>is</u> gone, he is dead
cop (fam): policeman ▶ **wrapped**: put round (to wrap)
you're a tough one (guy, man) (able to endure hardships)
mostly: almost all, chiefly ▶ **as far as I can see**: as much as I
can see ▶ **we'll get you to...**: we'll take you to...
absorbing: 'taking in', noticing

draw: produce a reaction ▶ **fire**: shooting (with his gun)
shoot at: fire a gun directed at; shoot sb dead
holding on to...: holding each other tightly ▶ **crying** (for joy)

glance: quick look; take a glance at ▶ **spotted**: fell on, noticed
hurried over: went over rapidly ▶ **claim**: get it (back) ▶ **even
though**: even if ▶ **be like Brenda**: be typical of... ▶ **remind him
that...**: make him remember that...

VOCABULARY

Voici environ 2 000 mots rencontrés dans la nouvelle, suivis du sens qu'ils ont dans celle-ci.

A

abduct enlever

about au sujet de, sur ; environ ; en, chez (qqn)

academically sur le plan scolaire

across de l'autre côté de

act agir

add ajouter

address s'adresser à

address book carnet d'adresses

adjoin être contigu à, toucher à

afraid of (be) avoir peur de

afterthought (as an) après coup, en y repensant

against contre

aging, ageing vieillissant

agree with être d'accord avec

agreement (be in) être d'accord

airy clair et spacieux

alcove recoin, renfoncement

alike semblable

alive vivant

all right bon, très bien

allow autoriser, permettre

all-pervasive qui se fait sentir partout, envahissant

almost presque

alone seul

aloud à haute voix ; fort

already déjà

alumni (sing. **alumnus**) anciens élèves

anger colère

angry en colère ; méchante (douleur), vilaine (cicatrice)

ankle cheville

annoyance irritation, agacement

antagonize contrarier, se mettre à dos

anxious impatient

anyhow de toute façon

anyplace (Am), **anywhere** n'importe où

apart différent, à l'opposé ; en morceaux, en pièces

apart (come) craquer (nerveusement)

apologetically d'un ton ou d'un air contrit

apologize s'excuser

appeal to attirer

arch one's back cambrer le dos

area région, zone

armoire (Am) placard

around aux environs de

as of, as from à partir de

as one comme un seul homme

as soon as dès que

as though, as if comme si

aside de côté

asleep endormi

assigned to (be) être désigné pour, être chargé de

assignment poste (d'affectation)

at most au plus

at that qui plus est, par-dessus le marché

attempt to tenter de, essayer de

attend assister à, être présent à

attendance assistance (nombre de gens présents)

attendant gardien, préposé

aunt tante

available disponible

avocation passe-temps favori, violon d'Ingres

avoid éviter

awake éveillé

awaken se réveiller

aware of conscient de

away (be) être absent, être parti

away from loin de
awfully terriblement, très

B
back arrière ; dos ; revers (de la main) ; en arrière
back (faire) reculer
back (get, got, got) retourner
background milieu, formation
backward(s) en arrière, vers l'arrière
badly mal
bald chauve
balding atteint de calvitie naissante
ballpoint pen stylo à bille
band bandeau
banner bannière
barely à peine
bark aboyer
bass perche (eau douce) ; loup, bar
bathroom salle de bains
battered endommagé, cabossé
bead perle, goutte
beard barbe
bearded barbu
beckon (to) faire signe (à)
become (became, become) devenir
bedspread dessus-de-lit
beep appeler au bip, biper
beg prier, supplier
begin (began, begun) commencer
behave se comporter
believe croire
belong on être à sa place, avoir sa place
belong to appartenir à
below dessous
bend virage
bend (bent, bent) down se pencher, se baisser
beneath sous
berserk fou furieux
beside à côté de, près de
bet (bet or betted, bet or betted) parier
betray trahir
better (had) faire mieux de
between entre

bewilder désorienter, abasourdir
beyond au-delà de
big thing of (make a) (faire semblant de) donner une grande importance à
bill (Am) billet de banque
bite (bit, bitten) mordre
blame sb for sth rejeter la responsabilité de qqch sur qqn
blank vierge, nu
blanket couverture
blazes ! diable !
blend (into) se fondre (dans), se mélanger (à)
blessing grâce, faveur, bénédiction
blink battre, cligner des paupières
block (Am) îlot, pâté de maisons
block letters (in) en majuscules, en lettres capitales
blood sang
blot out masquer, cacher
blotch tacher, marbrer
blouse chemisier
blow (blew, blown) souffler
blow up agrandir (photo)
blowup agrandissement (photo)
blue-flowered à fleurs bleues
bluejay geai
blunt brutal, (trop) direct
blur embuer, brouiller, troubler
board-up fermer, condamner
bolt verrou ; verrouiller
bolt upright droit comme un i
bone os
bookcase bibliothèque, rayonnages
booth box (café, restaurant)
born né ; **born teacher** professeur-né
bother déranger, ennuyer
bother doing sth prendre la peine de faire qqch
bother with s'intéresser à, faire cas de
bottom fond
bought ▶ buy
bounce faire des bonds
box boîte, carton
box number numéro de boîte postale

boyfriend petit ami
brag se vanter
brain cerveau
brake frein
break (broke, broken) casser ; interrompre ; se soustraire à
break loose détacher, arracher
break up se terminer
breaking point (be at the) être sur le point de craquer
breast sein
breath souffle, respiration
breathe respirer
breathless hors d'haleine
bride jeune mariée
bridegroom nouveau marié
briefcase serviette (mallette)
bright brillant, lumineux
bright (red) (rouge) vif
broad large
brought ► bring (brought, brought) apporter ; emmener
brown brun, marron
bruise contusionner, meurtrir
brush brosse ; accrochage (voiture) ; effleurer
brush off enlever
brush sb off écarter, repousser qqn
bucket seau
bud bourgeonner
budget (on a) au budget serré
build (built, built) up s'accroître
bullet balle (arme)
bump cahot ; cogner
bumpy accidenté, cahoteux
burly de forte carrure
burn (burnt or **burned, burnt** or **burned)** brûler ; cuire (douleur)
burst accès, éclat ; sursaut (d'énergie)
burst (burst, burst) éclater
burst into entrer en trombe
bury enterrer ; enfouir (souvenir...)
bush (rose ~) rosier
business affaire, entreprise, commerce
bustling animé
busy chargé (agenda, journée...) ; occupé, affairé

button (right on the) à l'heure pile, très exactement
buy (bought, bought) acheter
buzz bourdonner
by près de
by now à présent, maintenant

C

cab taxi ; **cab over** se rendre en taxi
cabin cabane
cabinet meuble de rangement
call appel ; appeler
call back rappeler (téléphone)
calm (down) calmer
can boîte de conserve
card table table de jeu
cardboard carton
care about se préoccuper de
care of (take, took, taken) prendre soin de, veiller sur
career carrière, métier ; **career day** journée d'orientation professionnelle
careful (be) faire attention
carefully avec soin ; prudemment
carpet(ing) moquette
carry porter, transporter
carry out mettre à exécution (menace...)
case affaire (droit) ; **be on a ~** enquêter sur une affaire
cash en espèces, comptant ; **~ register** caisse enregistreuse
casserole ragoût en cocotte
cast (cast, cast) jeter
catch prise de balle ; jeu de balle
catch (play) jouer à la balle
catch (caught, caught) up with rattraper (véhicule...) ; faire le point (avec qqn)
cater to (or for) pourvoir aux besoins de
catnap (take a) sommeiller, faire un (petit) somme
caught ► catch sb's attention retenir l'attention de qqn
cautiously prudemment
ceiling plafond
certainty certitude

chain enchaîner

chance chance, occasion, possibilité ; espoir

chance (take a) courir le risque

change se changer

chaperon chaperonner

chaperone (be the) faire office de chaperon

charge (take) prendre la situation en main

cheap bon marché ; de qualité médiocre

check (Am) addition (restaurant)

check contrôler

check on sb voir ce que fait qqn, surveiller qqn

cheek joue

cheer up réjouir, remonter le moral à

cheerful gai

chest poitrine

chicken casserole poulet à la cocotte

chill frisson, froid ; (se) refroidir, (se) rafraîchir

chilly frais, froid

china porcelaine

Chinese joint restaurant chinois (de bas étage)

choir chant choral ; chorale

choke étouffer ; s'étrangler (voix)

chore tâche

chose to ▶ choose to (chose, chosen) décider de, juger bon de

chuckle glousser

chunk gros morceau

churn bouillir intérieurement, fulminer

circle cercle

claim reprendre ; revendiquer, réclamer

clamp serrer ; fixer ensemble

clasp serrer, saisir

class (Am) (année de) promotion

class reunion réunion d'anciens élèves

classmate camarade de classe

clean propre

clean-shaven rasé de près

clear débarrasser (table) ; vider ; s'éclaircir (la gorge)

clear out se tirer, filer

clearing clairière

clearly de toute évidence, visiblement

clench serrer (dents, poings...)

clerk (Am) vendeur, vendeuse

click déclic ; petit bruit sec

clicking claquement, cliquetis

climb monter, grimper

cling (clung, clung) (to) coller (à), adhérer (à)

close (se) fermer ; se serrer (gorge)

close around se refermer sur

close to tout près de, contre

close-cropped coupé ras

closet (Am) penderie ; armoire, placard

cloth (morceau de) tissu, d'étoffe

clothes vêtements

clue indice

clump bouquet (d'arbres)

cluster se rassembler, se grouper

clutter with joncher de, surcharger de

coax from or **out of** obtenir par la cajolerie

coconut noix de coco

coffee shop cafétéria (restaurant)

coffeepot cafetière

college université, établissement d'enseignement supérieur

comb peigne

come across trouver, rencontrer

come back revenir

come by arriver, passer par là

come to think of it pendant que j'y pense

come up with trouver, découvrir ; avoir un plan

comfort réconforter

comfortable à l'aise, confortable

comment that faire la remarque que

commitment engagement

commode (Am) toilettes

company société

complete achever, terminer
concern inquiétude
concerned with préoccupé par
condo(minium) (appartement ou immeuble en) copropriété
confused troublé, embrouillé (esprit)
connection communication
considerate attentionné
conspicuous qui se fait remarquer
contact, contact lens lentille de contact
contemplative songeur, pensif
continuing ininterrompu, permanent
convincingly de manière convaincante
cook cuisinier, cuisinière
cook préparer (repas), cuisiner
cook up concocter, inventer (canular, histoire)
cool frais
cool off se calmer, se détendre
co-op apartement appartement en copropriété
copy exemplaire
corkboard panneau de liège
cost coût
costume jewelry bijoux fantaisie
cot (Am) lit de camp
cottage petite maison
couch canapé, divan
count on compter sur
count one's blessings s'estimer heureux
counter comptoir ; vitrine (pour bijoux)
county (Am) subdivision d'un Etat
couple of (a) deux ; quelques
coy rusé et coquet ; faussement timide, faussement effarouché
coyness fausse timidité
crack (open a door a ~) entrebâiller une porte
crash percuter
crazy (go) devenir fou
crazy about (be) raffoler de
creak grincer
cringe avoir un mouvement de recul, se faire tout petit

crisply sèchement
crook escroc, filou
cross traverser
crouch position accroupie ; s'accroupir
crowd foule
crowd around se rassembler autour de
crowded plein, bondé
crudely grossièrement, sommairement
crumple s'affaisser (au sol)
crunch (faire) crisser, craquer, grincer
crush on (have a) avoir le béguin pour
cry pleurer
cubicle cabine (d'essayage...)
cuddle cajoler
cuffs menottes
Cupid (play) jouer les Cupidons
curl boucler, friser
curly bouclé
curtained-off isolé, séparé par un rideau
curve faire une courbe ; courbe
cushion coussin
custody garde
customer client
cut (cut, cut) sb off couper la parole à qqn
cut through (the dumbness) tirer (de l'apathie)

D

daily quotidien
dame (Am) fille, nana
damn (fam) très, vachement
damn fool espèce d'idiot
damned (fam) vachement, terriblement, très
dangle pendre, pendiller
dare oser
dark glasses lunettes noires
dark grey gris foncé
darkness obscurité
dash (mad) course folle
dash se précipiter
date petit(e) ami(e)
date sb sortir avec qqn
dawn aube

day-by-day jour après jour
deal with traiter avec, avoir affaire à
dear life (for) pour sauver sa peau, de toutes ses forces
death sentence condamnation à mort
deathly mortel
decanter carafe
deceive tromper, abuser, duper
decipher déchiffrer
deep profond ; profondément
defeat vaincre, faire échouer
definite net, certain, incontestable
deftly habilement, adroitement
deli(catessen) épicerie fine
deliberate prudent, qui prend son temps
deliver distribuer ; livrer ; emmener, conduire
delivery distribution (poste) ; livraison
den (Am) petite pièce (confortable, isolée)
depth profondeur
desk bureau (meuble) ; réception (hôtel)
desk clerk réceptionniste
despair désespoir
desperately extrêmement ; désespérément
detective inspecteur (de police)
determined décidé, résolu
dial composer un numéro de téléphone
die mourir
dig (dug, dug) fouiller, creuser
dim faible (lumière)
direction directive, instruction
dirt road chemin de terre
disappear disparaître
disappearance disparition
disappointment déception
disbelief incrédulité
dislike ne pas aimer
disquieting inquiétant, alarmant, troublant
disturb the peace troubler l'ordre public
dizziness vertige(s)
dizzy (feel) avoir des vertiges
do (did, done) well réussir

dog-eared écorné
doorbell sonnette
doorway (in the) (dans) l'embrasure de la porte
dope personne stupide, bête
double pour deux
double-talk paroles trompeuses, langue de bois
doubt doute
doze off s'assoupir
drag oneself se traîner
draw (drew, drawn) attirer
drawer tiroir ; **top ~** le dessus du panier
dread frayeur ; redouter
dream rêve
dress s'habiller
dresser (Am) commode (avec miroir), coiffeuse
dressing-room cabine d'essayage
drew ▶ draw (drew, drawn) sortir, dégainer (arme)
drift aller à la dérive, dériver ; aller d'un pas nonchalant
drift in and out of sleep dormir d'un sommeil entrecoupé
drip dégoutter, dégouliner
drive trajet (en voiture)
drive (drove, driven) conduire ; aller en voiture
drive sb home raccompagner qqn en voiture
driver chauffeur, conducteur
driveway allée (menant à une maison)
droop s'affaisser
drop (laisser, faire) tomber ; déposer (en voiture)
drop back retomber
drop in passer voir
drowsy somnolent, ensommeillé
dry sec ; sécher
due back (be) devoir revenir (prévision)
due out (be) devoir sortir (prévision)
dug (dug, dug) into s'enfoncer dans
dump laisser tomber, plaquer
dye teindre

E

early premier (dans le temps) ; tôt

early thirties (be in one's ~) avoir entre 31 et 35 ans

earnest sérieux, appliqué ; grave

ease (at) ! du calme !

echo retentir, résonner

edge bord, limite ; pointe (d'agressivité... dans la voix...)

edge with border de

edgewise (get a word in) placer un mot

edgy nerveux, irritable

eerie mystérieux, inquiétant, sinistre

elderly d'un certain âge

elm tree orme

else (d') autre

elude échapper à

employee employé(e)

employer employeur

end bout, extrémité ; fin

end in se terminer par

enfold envelopper (dans ses bras)

engine moteur

engrossed in absorbé par, plongé dans

enjoy aimer, apprécier

entrance entrée

entry entrée (dans journal intime, dictionnaire...)

envision imaginer

errand course, commission

escape stairs escalier de secours

even régulier

even if même si

even so malgré tout, tout de même

eventually finalement

exhaustion extrême fatigue, épuisement

expect s'attendre à

explain expliquer

expressionless inexpressif ; monocorde (voix)

exquisite exquis ; raffiné, délicat, subtil

extended long, prolongé

extra (+ noun) supplémentaire

eye contact with (make) croiser le regard de qqn

eyelid paupière

F

face être en face de

factory usine

faculty corps enseignant

fade baisser (bruit) ; passer, se décolorer

faint léger, faible

fall (Am) automne

fall (fell, fallen) (se laisser) tomber

fall back to sleep se rendormir

fall in love with tomber amoureux de

fantasize fantasmer

fantasy imagination ; fantasme

fantasy life vie imaginaire

far loin

far (so) jusqu'à présent

farther plus loin

fast rapide ; vite, rapidement

fasten fixer, attacher

favour (do sb a) rendre un service à qqn

fear crainte

feature trait (visage)

fed up with (be) en avoir assez de, en avoir marre de

feel good être agréable ; faire du bien ; se sentir bien

feeling impression, sentiment

feet ► plur. de **foot** pied (30,48 cm)

fellow (fam) gars, type

fellow ! mon vieux !

felt ► feel (felt, felt) sentir ; ressentir

festive de fête

feverishly fébrilement

fifties (be in one's) avoir la cinquantaine

fight (have a) se quereller

fight (fought, fought) se battre

figure silhouette

figure chercher à comprendre, à trouver

figure out calculer, prévoir, préparer

file dossier ; classer, ranger ; déposer (rapport)
fill sb in on mettre qqn au courant de
fill with remplir de
find (found, found) trouver
fine (très) bien
fingertip bout du doigt
finish finition (peinture)
fire coup de feu
first premier ; en premier, d'abord
fish for chercher à dénicher
fist poing
fit convenir à
fix préparer (un repas) ; réparer
flashing clignotant
fleck petite tache, point
fleeting bref, éphémère
flesh chair
flicker lueur (d'espoir...)
fling (flung, flung) open ouvrir brusquement
flip over se retourner rapidement, complètement
flood of tears déluge de larmes
floor plancher ; sol ; étage
floorboard latte de plancher
floor-length qui va jusqu'au sol
flowered à fleurs
fly (flew, flown) voler (oiseau...)
fly mouche
flyer prospectus, poster
focus on (se) concentrer sur
fold pli ; (re)plier, ranger ; croiser (bras)
follow suivre ; venir après
follow up donner suite à
fool imbécile
foot (plur. **feet**) pied (30,48 cm)
forehead front
forestall empêcher, prévenir
forget (forgot, forgotten) oublier
fork embranchement
form (se) former
formal cérémonieux
former ancien (antérieur, d'autrefois)
forth en avant, vers l'avant
forties (in one's) d'une quarantaine d'années

forward vers l'avant, en avant
found ► **find (found, found)** trouver
four-letter word mot à cinq lettres
frame cadre ; encadrer
frame house maison en bois
frantically désespérément, comme un fou
free libérer, détacher
frenzy crise (de larmes...) ; frénésie, délire
fresh frais ; effronté
freshly récemment, nouvellement
fret se tracasser
friendly with (be) entretenir des relations amicales avec qqn
front of (in ~) devant
front window fenêtre de devant
frosty glacial
frown froncer les sourcils
frowning renfrogné, sombre
full plein (tarif...), total, complet
fume rager, fulminer
fun plaisir, amusement
fun of (make) se moquer de
funny bizarre, étrange
furnished meublé
furniture meubles
further autre, supplémentaire
fuss (with, over) faire grand cas (de)

G

gag bâillon
game partie (sport)
gas(oline) (Am) essence
gasp halètement ; haleter
gate barrière
gather supposer
gaunt décharné, très maigre
gave up ► **give (gave, given) up** abandonner, renoncer à
genuine authentique, réel
get (got, got) at atteindre
get away s'échapper, s'enfuir
get back revenir
get by se débrouiller, s'en tirer
get home rentrer chez soi
get on with continuer
get over passer (voir)

get sb to do sth persuader qqn de faire qqch
get sb's goat hérisser (qqn)
get up se lever
get (ou go) to sleep s'endormir
give (gave, given) donner
give out distribuer
glad content
glance at jeter un coup d'œil à
glance round jeter un coup d'œil circulaire
glasses (pair of) (paire de) lunettes
glimpse of (catch, get a ~) apercevoir, entrevoir
glisten briller ; luire
glitter scintiller, étinceler
glower at regarder avec colère
glue fixer, ne pas détacher (les yeux)
glum morose, sombre
gnawing lancinant, torturant
go (went, gone) along with être d'accord avec, accepter (plans, souhaits)
go back to (doing) se remettre (à faire)
go for s'enticher de, se toquer de
go over examiner
go to arriver à ; aller à
go through fouiller, examiner de près ; feuilleter
gone mort
gossip commérage
gossipy cancanier ; plein de potins
got back ▶ get (got, got) back revenir
gotta (I), (I) got to..., I have to... il faut que je...
gotten (Am) participe passé de **get**
gown robe (longue)
grab saisir ; voler, s'emparer de
graduate (Am) bachelier
graduate from sortir (avec diplôme) de
grand piano piano à queue
grant accorder, exaucer (souhait...)
grasp saisir

gratefully avec reconnaissance
graze effleurer, frôler
greasy gras, graisseux
great ! super ! génial !
grim sombre, sévère
grimy sale, crasseux
grip prise, étreinte ; saisir, empoigner
grip on oneself (get a ~) se contrôler, se maîtriser
groan gémir, grogner
ground sol
grove bosquet
grow (grew, grown) a beard laisser pousser sa barbe
grow to do sth se mettre à faire qqch
growing grandissant, qui augmente
grumpy grincheux
guess (Am) croire, penser, supposer
guest invité
guestroom chambre d'amis
guidance counsellor (Am) conseiller d'orientation
guilty coupable
gully ravine
gulp gorgée
gulp (in) avaler
gun pistolet, révolver
gut boyau, intestin ; **in one's gut** instinctivement
guy type
guys (Am) copains (garçons et filles) ; les gars ! les mecs !

H
hairspray laque
halt (bring to a) (faire) arrêter
halting hésitant (voix)
hammer donner des coups de marteau
hand passer, tendre
hand (at) à portée de main
hand (on the other ~) d'autre part
hand out distribuer
handcuff menotte
handle manche, poignée
handyman factotum
hang (hung, hung) onto s'accrocher à

hang (up) (sus)pendre ; **hang up on sb** raccrocher au nez de qqn

hanger porte-manteau, cintre

happen arriver (événement)

happen to be se trouver être...

hard dur

harden se durcir, se faire dur

hardly à peine

hardware store quincaillerie

harsh rêche, rugueux

hash hachis (plat en sauce à base de viande hachée et de légumes)

hate détester, haïr

have sb in faire venir qqn (pour exécuter un travail)

have sth to do with avoir un rapport avec

head tête, bout

head of (at the) à la tête de

head of hair chevelure

head for se diriger vers

headache mal de tête

hear (heard, heard) about entendre parler de

hear from avoir des nouvelles de

hearing, court hearing audience (tribunal)

heart-hunger cher à son cœur, chèrement désiré

heat up chauffer

heaven ciel, paradis

heavily abondamment, fortement ; lourdement

heavy lourd ; important, dense

heavyset trapu avec tendance à l'embonpoint

heels, **high heels** chaussures à (hauts) talons

help aide ; aider

helpful serviable, obligeant

helplessly sans pouvoir rien faire

here and now immédiatement, tout de suite

hex sort ; **put a ~ on sb** jeter un sort à qqn

hidden ▶ **hide (hid, hidden)** cacher, dissimuler

high (be) faire un trip (drogue)

high-heeled à talons hauts

high-pitched aigu (voix)

highly extrêmement, très

highway (Am) grande route, route nationale

hill colline

hiss dire d'une voix sifflante, siffler

hit (hit, hit) tomber sur, trouver ; heurter, frapper

hoax canular

hobble boitiller, clopiner

hold (held, held) back retenir

hold down maintenir couché, allongé

hold it ! attendez !

hollow caverneux (voix)

homeyness (Am) sentiment, impression d'être comme chez soi

honey (Am) (mon, ma) chéri(e)

honey-coloured couleur de miel

hook accrocher, fixer

hop in monter (dans une voiture...)

hope espoir ; espérer

hopeless sans espoir ; désespéré (cas, situation) ; inutile

hot (très) chaud

housewife ménagère

how come... ? comment se fait-il que... ?

hug serrer dans ses bras

hunch intuition

hung around ▶ **hang (hung, hung) around** traînailler, être par là

hungry (be) avoir faim

hurriedly précipitamment

hurry faire se dépêcher

hurry (be in a) être pressé

hurry up se dépêcher

hurt (hurt, hurt) blesser, faire mal

hurtle foncer, avancer à toute allure

hurtle past passer en trombe

I

ice bucket seau à glace

identify oneself se nommer

ignore ignorer, ne pas tenir compte de

ill malade

illegible illisible

impassive impassible

impulse (on) dans un élan

inch pouce (2,54 cm)

inconspicuous qui passe inaperçu

indulge oneself in se faire plaisir avec, s'offrir (le luxe de)

inside à l'intérieur (de), dans ; ~ **pocket** poche intérieure

instantly immédiatement

instead (of) au lieu (de)

intently (très) attentivement

intone déclamer

introduce sb to sb else présenter qqn à qqn d'autre

involve impliquer

inwardly intérieurement

issue question, problème

J

jacket veste

jagged irrégulier, dentelé

jail prison

jingle tinter, cliqueter

jitters (have the) être nerveux, avoir le trac

join se joindre à, participer à ; relier

joint boui-boui (café, restaurant)

jot down prendre note de

joyfully joyeusement

jump sauter ; sursauter

jump out at sauter aux yeux de

junk bric-à-brac, vieilleries, ferraille

K

keen vif, fort, intense

keep (kept, kept) garder, tenir, retenir

keep (on) continuer ; ~ **doing** continuer à faire

keep from empêcher de

keep in touch with rester en relation avec

keep track of sb se tenir au courant de ce que fait qqn

keep up continuer, poursuivre

keeper gardien

key clef ; touche (piano...)

keyring porte-clefs

kick donner un coup de pied

kid enfant ; gosse

kill tuer

kind bon, bienveillant

kind sorte

kind of plus ou moins, un peu

kindly bienveillant

klutz (Am) empoté, manche

knee genou

knock frapper (à la porte)

knot nœud

know (knew, known) savoir, connaître ; comprendre, se rendre compte

L

laboured pénible, laborieux

lace dentelle

laid out ▶ lay (laid, laid) out disposer

lake lac

lane chemin, ruelle

lap genoux, giron

large grand, spacieux

last dernier ; ~ **night** hier soir ; **at** ~ enfin

late en retard

late afternoon (in the ~) vers la fin de l'après-midi

lately récemment

laugh rire

laughter rire (noun)

launch se lancer (dans un discours...)

laundry linge (propre ou sale)

law loi

lay (laid, laid) down fixer, établir (loi, règle) ; disposer

lead (led, led) mener, conduire

lean maigre

lean (leant or **leaned, leant** or **leaned)** se pencher

leaped ▶ leap (leapt or **leaped, leapt** or **leaped)** sauter, bondir

learn (learnt or **learned, learnt** or **learned)** apprendre

least (at) au moins

leave on laisser branché

leave sth around laisser traîner, **(deliberately)** disposer
leaves (sing. **leaf**) branches
left (on the) (à) gauche
left ► leave (left, left) laisser, quitter
left out ► leave (left, left) out ne pas prendre
leftover restant, qui reste
lemon citron ; ruine, voiture invendable
lemonade (Am) citron pressé
lend (lent, lent) prêter
lens lentille
let (let, let) laisser, permettre
let go lâcher
let in faire entrer, laisser entrer
let sb in on sth mettre qqn au courant de qqch (secret)
let slip by laisser passer
let up on sb lâcher la bride à qqn
lettering caractères (lettres)
level niveau
license plate (Am) plaque d'immatriculation
lid couvercle
lie (lay, lain) être couché, être allongé
lift (up) soulever
light léger
light-brown brun clair
light-headedness étourdissement
lights (red) feux (rouges)
like (be) être typique de (qqn)
lilt inflexions (dans la voix), rythme, cadence
line gamme (de produit) ; ride
lingering long, insistant
lip lèvre
listen for guetter (un bruit...)
lively vif
loads of une flopée de, des tas de
loafer mocassin
lobby hall d'entrée
location ► on location job mission
lock serrure
lonely seul, esseulé
loner (a) (un) solitaire
long as (as) tant que
longingly avec envie

look air, mine, aspect ; regard
look sembler, avoir l'air
look ! écoutez !
look at (take a) jeter un coup d'œil à (pour réparer)
look for chercher
look into enquêter sur, examiner, étudier
look like ressembler
looks beauté ; apparences
loop nouer ; boucle
loose desserré, détaché
loosen détacher, libérer
lost ► lose (lost, lost) perdre
lot (a) beaucoup
lot, parking lot (Am) parking
loudly d'une voix forte
lousy très mal à l'aise
love adorer (qqch)
lover amoureux
low-cut décolleté
lower baisser, abaisser
luck chance
lull accalmie
lumpy défoncé, bosselé
lurk rôder

M
mad fou
mad at furieux contre
made ► make (made, made) faire, gagner (de l'argent)
madness folie
magnifying glass loupe
mail (Am) courrier ; envoyer, expédier
main principal
make atteindre (lieu), arriver
make eyes at faire les yeux doux à
make out déchiffrer ; distinguer
make up compenser, rattraper
makeshift de fortune
makeup (nécessaire) de maquillage
makings (sandwiches ~) de quoi faire des sandwiches
mall (shopping ~) centre commercial, galerie marchande

manacle menotte ; mettre les menottes

manage to (do) réussir à (faire)

mansion château, manoir ; hôtel particulier

map carte routière

match être assorti à

matter importer (avoir de l'importance)

matter how (no ~) peu importe comment

matter of fact (as a ~) en fait

mattress matelas

maybe peut-être

meal repas

mean (meant, meant) signifier, vouloir dire

mean it ne pas plaisanter, être sérieux

meantime (in the ~) entre-temps

measure mesurer

medium milieu ; **7 medium** taille 39 en chaussures

meeting réunion, rencontre

memory souvenir ; mémoire

Mercantile Exchange (New York) Bourse des marchandises de New York

mercilessly sans pitié, impitoyablement

met ▶ meet (met, met) rencontrer ; faire la connaissance de

middle milieu

middle-aged d'âge mûr, d'un certain âge

mighty puissant, fort ; gros (effort...)

mind esprit ; **in ~** à l'esprit

mind (change one's ~) changer d'avis

mingle mélanger, mêler

minute... (the) dès l'instant où...

mirror refléter

miserable méprisable

miss manquer, rater ; regretter l'absence de

miss (not to) ne pas manquer (de voir), bien remarquer

missing disparu ; manquant

missing person's report avis de recherche (pour disparu)

mistake erreur, faute

mistake (mistook, mistaken) se méprendre sur

misunderstanding malentendu

mix mélanger ; préparation ; (se) mêler, (se) mélanger

moist légèrement humide

moisten one's lips s'humecter les lèvres

moment instant

most (of) la majeure partie de ; la plupart (de)

mother-of-pearl nacre

mouth bouche

move déménagement ; déménager ; (se) déplacer, bouger

move up avancer (changer date)

mover déménageur

mud-coloured de couleur terne

muddy terne, pâle (couleur)

mug chope

muggy humide et lourd (temps)

mumble marmonner

murder assassiner, tuer

murderer assassin, meurtrier

muslin mousseline

mutter grommeler ; marmonner

N

nail clouer

named du nom de

narrow étroit ; se rétrécir ; plisser (yeux)

near sur le point de, près de ; presque (dans mots composés)

near s'approcher de, être au bord de

nearby proche, avoisinant

neardark pénombre

nearly presque

near-panic (in ~) au bord de la panique

neatly soigneusement, impeccablement

neatness (sens de l') ordre, propreté

need avoir besoin de

needle aiguille

neighbouring avoisinant, proche

nevertheless cependant, néanmoins

news nouvelles (radio...)

next prochain, suivant
next to à côté de, près de
next to last avant-dernier
nibble grignoter
nice-looking beau
night before last avant-hier soir
nightgown chemise de nuit
nightstand table table de nuit
nod faire signe de la tête (approbation)
noisy bruyant
none aucun(e)
no-nonsense qui ne plaisante pas, sérieux
nonsense non-sens, inepties
noon midi
nope non
notation note (écrite)
note mot (écrit)
notebook carnet ; **student ~** cahier d'écolier
notice annonce, avis ; remarquer, s'apercevoir de
nudge pousser légèrement (du coude)
numb engourdi
numbly avec un air hébété
numbness engourdissement ; torpeur
nurse soigner
nursery chambre d'enfants

O
oak chêne
obedience obéissance ; **in ~ to** conformément à
obey sb obéir à qqn
obvious évident
occur to venir à l'esprit de
odd étrange, bizarre ; **~ jobs** petits travaux, petits boulots
odyssey odyssée, récit
off by oneself à l'écart
offer to proposer de
office bureau (pièce)
oil changed (have the) faire faire la vidange
old days (in the) autrefois
once une fois
one seul et unique
only seul (et unique)
open (s') ouvrir

open into donner sur
opening ouverture, passage
opposite en face de, devant
or so à peu près, environ
order commande ; **place an ~** passer commande
order commander (qqch) ; donner un ordre
otherwise sinon, autrement
outburst flambée, accès
outdoor de plein air
outing excursion, randonnée
outline contour
outrage indignation
outside dehors, à l'extérieur
oven four
over au cours de, pendant ; au sujet de, à propos de ; au-dessus (de) ; par-dessus ; plus de
over fini, terminé
over (all) partout
over and over (again) d'une façon répétée
overcoat pardessus
overgrown trop grand, géant
overhead au-dessus (de) ; **~ light** plafonnier
overlook donner sur
overnight bag petit sac de voyage
overpower avoir le dessus sur
overstuffed rembourré à craquer
owe devoir (argent)
own propre, personnel
owner propriétaire

P
pack faire ses bagages
package paquet
padlock cadenas ; cadenasser
pain douleur
pains to do (take) se donner de la peine pour faire
paint maquiller
panel panneau
panic s'affoler
parch dessécher
park garer
parlour (pizza ~) pizzeria
parole liberté conditionnelle ; **~ officer** contrôleur judiciaire

partition cloison
partly en partie
partner associé
partnership partenariat, état d'associé
pass out faire circuler, distribuer
past au-delà de ; passé
patch plaque, coin, endroit
path allée, chemin
patrolman (Am) policier
pause s'interrompre
peace paix
peaceful paisible, calme
peal sonner
peel s'écailler
peer at regarder attentivement, scruter
pencil crayon ; écrire au crayon
perfect parfait
perspiration transpiration, sueur
phone back rappeler
phone book annuaire (du téléphone)
phone in sth communiquer qqch par téléphone
photographer photographe
pick out repérer
pick up aller chercher (en voiture) ; arrêter (malfaiteur) ; ramasser
picture photo ; imaginer, se figurer
pile tas
pillow oreiller
pillowcase taie d'oreiller
pin épingle
pin to épingler, attacher à
pit creux (de l'estomac)
pitcher pichet
placate calmer, apaiser
place endroit ; placer, disposer
plan projet ; projeter, établir un plan
plant usine
plaster coller
plate assiette ; plaque (d'immatriculation...)
play passer (disque, cassette...) ; jouer
play button mise en marche ; « lecture » (appareil)
plead supplier, implorer

pleasant agréable
pleased content, satisfait
plug connecter, brancher
point (the) l'essentiel
point in (there is no ~) il ne sert à rien de
point out désigner (du doigt) ; faire remarquer
poke fourrer, enfoncer
pole (telephone) poteau téléphonique
polish astiquer ; cirer
pollute polluer
porch (Am) véranda
position poste
post afficher
poster-sized de la taille d'une affiche
pot of coffee (make a) faire du café
pound livre (454 g)
pound piler, battre, frapper
pour verser
practise répéter, s'exercer à
pray prier
preacher (Am) pasteur
pregnant (with) enceinte (de)
present cadeau
press appuyer sur ; insister
pretend to faire semblant de
pretty assez, plutôt, passablement
pretty joli
prickle fourmiller, picoter
pride orgueil ; fierté
prim très convenable, très comme il faut
primary principal
print tirage, épreuve (photo) ; imprimer
print dress robe imprimée
private investigator détective privé
produce présenter, sortir, montrer
prom (Am) bal d'élèves ou d'étudiants
promise jurer, promettre
properly convenablement, correctement
prosecutor procureur
protect protéger

proudly fièrement
puff souffler
pull tirer
pull away démarrer, s'en aller
pull in se garer, s'arrêter
pull loose détacher (en tirant), libérer
pull off arracher
pull oneself up se redresser
pull up s'arrêter (véhicule)
purple violet
purse serrer, pincer (lèvres)
push down contenir, maîtriser, réduire
push on (fam) aller
put (put, put) back remettre
put in installer
put on mettre (vêtement)
puzzle rendre perplexe

Q

queen reine
quickly rapidement
quiet calme, paisible ; silencieux
quiver trembler

R

race aller très vite
race down parcourir rapidement (liste)
rack portant (pour vêtements)
raincoat imperméable
raise lever
rap donner un coup sec
rattle faire un bruit de ferraille, cliqueter
raw à l'état pur (émotion)
ray rayon
reach atteindre ; atteinte, portée
read (read, read) (se) lire
real (Am), **really** vraiment, réellement
realize se rendre compte
receiver combiné téléphonique ; **put the ~ down** raccrocher
recipient destinataire
reckless téméraire, imprudent
recognize reconnaître
recorder appareil enregistreur
recreation room salle de jeux
refer to parler de, faire référence à

reflect réfléchir (mûrement)
register (s') inscrire, (s') enregistrer ; exprimer (sentiment)
reject rejeter, éliminer
relationship relation, rapport
release soulagement ; libérer (prisonnier...) ; détacher
relentlessly implacablement, inexorablement
relief soulagement
reluctance réticence
reluctant fait à regret, à contre-cœur
reluctantly à contre-cœur
remind sb of sth rappeler qqch à qqn
remotely vaguement ; **not ~** pas le moins du monde
remove ôter, enlever
removed from éloigné de
rent louer ; **rented apartment** meublé
repair réparation ; **~ service** service de dépannage
repairman réparateur
replace remplacer
report rapport
report sb missing porter qqn disparu
report to se présenter à
request demande
respond to réagir à
rest se reposer ; reposer (sur...)
restless agité
retire prendre sa retraite
retirement retraite
reunion retrouvailles, réunion
reward récompense
rewound ► rewind (rewound, rewound) rembobiner
rid of (get) se débarrasser de
riddled with criblé de
ride trajet (en voiture...)
ride (give sb a) emmener qqn en voiture...
right tout à fait, complètement, très ; qui convient
right droit (n)
right (be) avoir raison
right (make a) tourner à droite
right (on the, to the ~) à droite, vers la droite

right away immédiatement, tout de suite

right back (be) revenir tout de suite

right here ici même

right now immédiatement

ring anneau ; sonnerie

ring (rang, rung) sonner

rip (se) fendre, (se) déchirer

roar rugir, vrombir

robbery vol

robe robe de chambre, peignoir

roll pellicule photo ; petit pain ; rouler

room place (de la), espace

root racine

rose ► rise (rose, risen) se lever

rot (away) pourrir ; se délabrer

rotten pourri ; minable, moche

rough brutal, violent ; rêche

rough it vivre à la dure

round rond(e)

Route 80 la Nationale 80

row dispute

rub frotter

rubber caoutchouc

rug carpette, petit tapis

rugged costaud, viril

rumble gronder (bruit) ; gargouiller

rumple froisser

run (ran, run) late être en retard

run sb off (the road) forcer qqn à quitter la route

run out tirer à sa fin, s'épuiser (temps...)

run through passer (la main... dans les cheveux...)

rush se précipiter

rust rouille

rustic grossier, non raffiné ; champêtre

rusty rouillé

S

sachet bag sachet ; berlingot

sad triste

safe en sécurité

safety catch cran de sécurité

sagging affaissé, défoncé

sale vente

salesclerk (Am) vendeur, vendeuse

sang ► sing (sang, sung) chanter

sat up ► sit (sat, sat) up se dresser sur son séant

saunter aller d'un pas nonchalant, flâner

save économiser

saw ► see (saw, seen) voir

say dites donc, dites-moi

say (said, said) dire

scant 30 minutes (a) 30 minutes à peine

school-kid écolier

scrap petit morceau (de papier)

scratch gratter

scrawl griffonnage, gribouillage

scream crier

screech émettre un bruit strident, hurler

screen door porte munie d'une moustiquaire

screw vis

screwdriver tournevis

scribble griffonner (à la hâte)

scrub nettoyer à la brosse

search fouiller

search for chercher

searing cuisant (douleur)

seated assis

security guard vigile

seem sembler, paraître

select choisir

self (be one's) être soi-même

self-justifying d'autojustification, justificatif

semi-dark pénombre

senior (Am) élève de terminale

sense sens, sentiment, conscience ; sentir (intuitivement), deviner

sentence condamnation

serve purger (une peine)

set (television ~) poste de télévision ; série

set (set, set) placer, mettre ; figer

set (have one's hair ~) se faire faire une mise en plis

set down poser, déposer

set in commencer, s'installer

set out mettre, disposer
set up implanter (une usine...)
settle (oneself) s'installer
shabby minable, misérable
shackle enchaîner, attacher
shackles chaînes, fers
shade ton, nuance (couleurs)
shadow ombre
shadowy flou, indistinct
shaggy à longs poils ; broussailleux
shake (shook, shaken) hands with serrer la main à
share partager
sharp pointu
sharply brusquement, vivement ; nettement
shave se raser
sheer très fin, transparent
sheet drap ; feuille (papier) ; ~ **music** partition
shelves (sing. **shelf**) étagères, rayonnages (livres)
shine (shone, shone) briller
shirt chemise
shoe chaussure
shoelace lacet de chaussure
shone ► **shine**
shook ► **shake (shook, shaken)** secouer
shoot prendre en photo
shoot (shot, shot) at tirer sur
shooting lancinant (douleur)
shortcut raccourci
short-sleeved à manches courtes
shorts short
shot ► **shoot**
shoulder épaule
shout cri ; s'écrier
shove pousser (sans ménagement)
showed ► **show (showed, shown)** montrer, dévoiler ; être visible
shower douche ; prendre une douche
shrank ► **shrink (shrank, shrunk) back** reculer en se faisant tout petit
shred déchiqueter ; lambeau

shriek cri perçant ; hurler, pousser un cri perçant
shut (shut, shut) fermer
shutter volet
shuttered aux volets fermés
shyly timidement
sick malade ; **out** ~ en arrêt maladie
sick of (be) en avoir marre de
sick worry inquiétude folle
sickened écœuré
side côté, flanc ; ~ **door** porte latérale
sigh soupirer
sight vue
sign enseigne, panneau
sign up s'inscrire
signal faire signe
silly stupide, sot, bête
silver argent
sink (Am) W.C.
sip boire à petites gorgées, siroter
size taille (vêtements...)
sketch faire un tableau rapide de
skim parcourir rapidement, feuilleter
skimpy peu abondant, maigre
skin peau
skinny maigrichon
skirt jupe ; longer, contourner
skull crâne
slack jeu, mou
slacks pantalon (de sport)
slam claquer (porte) ; ~ **on the brakes** freiner à fond ; ~ **the phone down** raccrocher brutalement
slanting oblique
slap donner une tape (dans le dos)
sleep (slept, slept) dormir
sleepiness envie de dormir
sleeping bag sac de couchage
sleepless night nuit blanche
slender élancé, mince
slice tranche
slide (slid, slid) (se) glisser
slight léger, faible
slightly légèrement

slip (from) glisser (hors de) ; (se) glisser (discrètement)

slippery glissant ; visqueux

slob cochon, gros porc (injurieux)

slow (down) ralentir

slowness lenteur

sluggishness mollesse, lenteur, léthargie

smash fracasser, briser (en frappant fort)

smell (smelt or **smelled, smelt** or **smelled)** sentir

smile at sourire à

smooth lisser

smoulder couver ; **~ with jealousy** se consumer de jalousie

snap dire sèchement ; prendre un instantané ; se casser net ou avec un bruit sec

snap on allumer d'un geste brusque

snapshot instantané (photo)

sneak se déplacer à pas furtifs

sneaker (chaussure de) tennis, basket

snicker ricanement ; rire en dessous

snoop around fureter, fouiner

snore ronfler

snort grogner

soak tremper

sob sangloter

sock chaussette

socket orbite

soft doux

soil salir, souiller

sold ► sell (sold, sold) vendre

sole semelle

solicitously avec sollicitude

somehow pour une raison ou pour une autre ; d'une façon ou d'une autre

someplace (Am) quelque part

soon tôt ; bientôt

sorrow chagrin

soul âme (qui vive)

sound like ressembler (à l'entendre)

soundless silencieux

sour amer, aigre

space (parking ~) place de stationnement

spacey (be) planer complètement (drogue)

sparkle briller, étinceler

speed vitesse

spent ► spend (spent, spent) passer (temps) ; dépenser (argent)

spirit esprit

spot repérer ; endroit, place ; poste ; tache ; **on the ~** sur-le-champ, immédiatement

spread couvre-lit

spring printemps ; ressort

sprinkler arrosoir rotatif

squad escouade ; **~ car** voiture de police

squarely carrément, franchement

squawk cri rauque

squeal crissement

squint regarder en clignant

stack tas, pile ; empiler, entasser

staff personnel

stain tacher, souiller

stake on miser sur, risquer sur

stalk régner sur

stall (for time) gagner du temps

stance position, attitude

stand (stood, stood) se tenir debout ; supporter

stare regard fixe ; regarder fixement

start faire démarrer (voiture...) ; commencer

starter démarreur

starting with commençant par

startle faire sursauter

startled très surpris

State High (school) (Am) lycée

statement déclaration, déposition

station gare

stay rester ; séjourner

steadily régulièrement

steady régulier, constant

steady oneself rétablir son équilibre

steer faire route vers ; diriger

step faire un ou des pas, marcher ; marchepied

stick (stuck, stuck) coller

stick oneself venir se fourrer (dans un endroit)

stiff raide

stifle étouffer

stifling suffocant (chaleur)

still encore, toujours ; silencieux ; faire taire, étouffer

stink (stank, stunk) clocher, sentir l'arnarque ; puer

stinking sacré, foutu

stitch point, maille ; (par extension) vêtement

stomp aller d'un pas lourd et bruyant

stood up ▶ **stand (stood, stood) up** se lever, se mettre debout

stop (come to a ~) s'arrêter, s'immobiliser

stop by passer voir

store (Am), **shop** magasin, boutique

story histoire (fabriquée de toutes pièces)

straggly désordonné, en désordre

straight sans détour, très franchement

straighten redresser, ajuster ; ~ **out** arranger, mettre de l'ordre dans

straighten up se redresser

strain tendre fortement ; plisser (les yeux)

stranger étranger, inconnu

streak strie

streaked (have one's hair ~) se faire faire des mèches

stressed stressé

stretch tendre, étirer

stride grand pas, enjambée

strike (struck, struck) frapper

string corde (piano) ; ficelle

strip (se) déshabiller

striped rayé, à rayures, tigré

stroke attaque (d'apoplexie)

struck ▶ **strike**

stubble of beard barbe de plusieurs jours

stuff (fam) affaires, choses, trucs

stuff fourrer ; ~ **with** bourrer de

stumble trébucher

stunt (pull a) faire un coup (bon ou mauvais)

substantial important

suburban de banlieue

suburbanite (souvent péjoratif) banlieusard

sue intenter un procès à

sugary sucré

suit costume

suitable qui convient

suitcase valise

summon faire venir, appeler

sunglasses lunettes de soleil

sunny ensoleillé

sure (Am) sûrement, assurément

sure (make) s'assurer

surround entourer

suspect soupçonner

suspicious suspect

swagger démarche assurée ; air fanfaron

swallow avaler ; ~ **back** ravaler

sway (se) balancer ; osciller

swear (swore, sworn) être certain ; jurer

sweat sueur

sweetheart chéri(e)

swell (swelled, swollen or swelled) enfler, gonfler

swift rapidement

swim (swam, swum) nager

swing balançoire

swing (swung, swung) balancer

switchboard standard ; ~ **operator** standardiste

swollen gonflé, enflé

sympathetic compatissant

T

tack clou, pointe ; fixer sur un support

tackle plaquer (rugby, football américain) ; saisir (à bras-le-corps)

tag étiquette

take (took, taken) away enlever, emmener

take back to reconduire, ramener à

take in noter (détail...), observer

take on prendre en charge, accepter (responsabilité...)

take sb up on sth prendre qqn au mot, accepter l'offre... de qqn

taken off ▶ take off enlever, ôter ; partir

take-out repas à emporter

talk parler

talk it out mettre les choses au clair

tape cassette ; bande magnétique ; attacher (avec du scotch)

task besogne, tâche

taste goût

taught ▶ teach (taught, taught) enseigner

taut raide, tendu

tear déchirure ; larme

tear (tore, torn) (se) déchirer

tease taquiner

teddy bear nounours, ours en peluche

teenage adolescence

teenager adolescent

teeth dents (sing. **tooth**)

telephone operator's station standard téléphonique

tell (told, told) savoir, se rendre compte

term trimestre (scolaire)

terrific formidable, fantastique

tersely laconiquement, de manière concise

testy irritable

thee (archaic) vous, toi

therefore par conséquent

thick gros, épais

thin mince ; se réduire, s'amenuiser

think a lot of tenir en haute estime

third troisième

thought pensée, idée

thought of ▶ think (thought, thought) of penser à

thoughtful songeur, pensif, sérieux ; attentionné

threat menace ; menacer

threw back ▶ throw (threw, thrown) back renvoyer (balle...)

throat gorge

through à travers

throughout partout dans ; pendant toute la durée de

throw on enfiler rapidement (vêtement)

thump bruit sourd ; frapper fort

tie attacher, nouer

tight juste, serré (vêtement)

tighten serrer ; se resserrer

tightly fermement, bien fort

time fois

time (at one) à une certaine époque, autrefois

time (by the) quand

times (at) par moments, parfois

tin étain

tingle (with) piquer, picoter (de)

tiny tout petit, minuscule

tip extrémité, pointe

tiptoe aller sur la pointe des pieds

tire (Am), tyre pneu

tired fatigué

tiresome ennuyeux

toaster grille-pain

tone ton (de la voix)

tonelessly sans timbre, atone

tongue langue

tonight ce soir

too aussi, également ; qui plus est

took (to, through...) ▶ take (took, taken) to, through mener à

took out ▶ take out sortir

took over ▶ take over succéder, suivre

tool outil

top sommet, haut

top drawer le dessus du panier

top of (on ~) sur le dessus de, sur

topple (faire) basculer, (faire) tomber

toss jeter négligemment ; lancer

touch note, touche

touch with (in) en contact avec

tough dur à cuire

tour visiter (faire du tourisme)
towards vers, en direction de ; aux environs de
towell serviette (de table)
toy jouet
track down traquer, retrouver
trader négociant, opérateur (en Bourse)
trail off se taire peu à peu (voix)
trespass transgresser (propriété...)
trespassing (no) défense d'entrer
trickle filet (d'eau, de sang...)
tried ▶ try essayer
trigger stimuler, déclencher
trim net, soigné, coquet ; mince, svelte
trip voyage ; excursion
trouble problèmes, difficultés, ennuis
trousers pantalon
trust faire confiance à
try essayer ; ~ **on** essayer (vêtement)
tuck rentrer ; border ; ~ **sb in** border qqn
tug tirer
tug to (give a) tirer sur
tune (out of) désaccordé
turn tour (de clef)
turn around faire pivoter
turn down rejeter, refuser ; rabattre
turn-off bretelle d'accès, embranchement, sortie
turn on brancher
turn out se révéler (être) ; venir, se présenter (en grand nombre)
turn out fine s'arranger
turn over se retourner
twice deux fois
twin jumeau, jumelle
twirl tournoyer
twist zigzaguer, serpenter ; (se) tordre ; visser
twisting sinueux

U

unabashed sans retenue, dont on n'a pas honte

unaware of inconscient de
unconsciously inconsciemment
uncork déboucher
underneath sous, au-dessous de
understandable compréhensible
underwear sous-vêtements
undo (undid, undone) desserrer, défaire
uneasily avec gêne
uneasy agité (sommeil)
uneven inégal, irrégulier
unfamiliar inconnu
unfasten détacher
unforgiving impitoyable
ungrateful ingrat
unheeding of indifférent à
unit local
unlock ouvrir (avec une clef) ; défaire, détacher
unrestrained effréné, sans retenue
unshaven pas rasé
unsnap ouvrir d'un coup sec
unsure incertain
unusual inhabituel
unwilling involontaire, malgré soi
up (be) être en forme
up to jusqu'à ; à la hauteur de
upholstery tissu d'ameublement
upright droit ; ~ **piano** piano droit
upset agacé, contrarié
upset (upset, upset) émouvoir ; bouleverser
urgency insistance
use se servir de, utiliser
use doing (no) inutile de faire
usher (into) introduire, faire entrer dans
usual habituel ; **as** ~ comme d'habitude
utterly complètement

V

vacation (Am) vacances
van camionnette
vanish disparaître
vanquish vaincre

variety of (a) un certain nombre de

VCR (video cassette recorder) magnétoscope

veer virer

velour(s) velours épais

veneer placage, revêtement

vent ventilateur ; ventilation

vestige trace, brin

veto opposer son veto à

vexation contrariété, tracas

viewpoint point de vue

volunteer dire spontanément, de soi-même

vote voter ; **vote sb into partnership** prendre qqn comme associé (par vote)

vow vœu, serment

W

wad liasse

waffle gaufre

wail gémir

wailing hurlement (sirène)

waist taille (corps)

wait for (sb, sth) attendre (qqn, qqch)

waitress serveuse (restaurant)

walk marcher

walk out of quitter en signe de désapprobation

walk out on sb quitter, plaquer qqn

wall mur

wallpaper tapisserie, papier peint

warm chaleureux

warn avertir

warning avertissement

waste déchets ; gaspillage ; gaspiller (temps, argent)

watch regarder ; observer

wave vague

way manière, façon ; **that ~** de cette façon

way to (on the ~) en allant à

waylay (waylaid, waylaid) guetter et agresser

wear (wore, worn) porter (vêtement)

wedding mariage, noces ; **~ brunch** (Am) or **supper**

repas de noces ; **~ gown** robe de mariée

weep (wept, wept) pleurer

weight poids

weird mystérieux, bizarre, inquiétant

weld souder

well monter (larmes)

well-kept soigné, bien entretenu

wet humide, mouillé

wheel (steering) volant

wheeze respiration sifflante ; respirer avec difficulté ou bruyamment

whenever chaque fois que

whereabouts où (est qqn) ; **know sb's ~** savoir où est qqn

while espace de temps ; pendant que ; tandis que

whip off enlever brusquement

whirl around pivoter, tourbillonner

whir vrombir

whirring vrombissement

whisper murmure ; murmurer

whistling sifflant

whiten blanchir ; blêmir

whole entier, complet

wide spacieux

wide (open a door) ouvrir grand une porte

wide-pupilled aux pupilles dilatées

wig perruque

wiggle faire bouger, agiter, remuer

wild-looking fantaisiste, fou

wildly comme un fou, l'air très agité

wild rice riz sauvage

will sb to do sth adjurer intérieurement qqn de faire qqch

willing disposé (à faire)

wind (wound, wound) around combiner, caser entre

window, **store ~** (Am), **shop ~** vitrine

windowpane carreau

wink clin d'œil

wink of (not a) pas le moindre

wire fil (métallique ou de fer) ; ressort (canapé)

wish souhait

wistful mélancolique, nostalgique

withdrawn renfermé

within dans ; avant la fin de

witness témoin

wobble branler, lâcher peu à peu

woke up ▶ **wake (woke** or **waked, woken** or **waked) up** se réveiller

wonder se demander

wood bois

word parole (de chanson) ; parole, promesse

wore ▶ **wear**

work marcher, fonctionner

work one's way... arriver progressivement (à ...)

work out well s'arranger

work up provoquer, susciter, stimuler ; mettre au point

workshop atelier

worktable établi

worried inquiet

worry inquiétude ; s'inquiéter

worth (be) valoir ; valoir la peine

wrap envelopper

wreck (old) (vieille) guimbarde

wreck détruire, abîmer

wrinkle (se) froisser ; (se) rider

wrist poignet

write (wrote, written) up faire un compte rendu de

wrong (sth) qqch qui ne va pas

Y

yank arracher ; tirer d'un coup sec ; ~ **on** enfiler rapidement (vêtement) ; ~ **shut** fermer d'un coup sec

yard unité de longueur (91,44 cm)

yell hurler

yield céder

Achevé d'imprimer en novembre 2010 en France sur Presse Offset par
Maury-Imprimeur - 45330 Malesherbes
N° d'imprimeur : 158730
Dépôt légal 1ʳᵉ publication : avril 2002
Édition 05 - novembre 2010
Librairie Générale Française - 31, rue de Fleurus - 75278 Paris Cedex 06

30/8691/5